STORIES FROM A JOKE THIEF

by Buddy Stein

4/22/05

Enjoy the book

Buddy Stein

Stories From a Joke Thief

Published by Hats Off Books™
610 East Delano Street, Suite 104, Tucson, Arizona 85705 U.S.A.

www.hatsoffbooks.com
Edited by Claire Gerus Klein, Tucson, Arizona
Cover design by Gayle Miller, Athens, Greece

Publisher's Cataloging-in-Publication
(Provided by Quality Books, Inc.)

Stein, Buddy, 1931-
Stories from a joke thief / by Buddy Stein.
p. cm.
LCCN 2005921629
ISBN 1587364522

1. Stein, Buddy, 1931- 2. Comedians--United States--Biography. 3. Stand-up comedy--United States.
I. Title.

PN2287.S6775A3 2005 792.7'028'092
QBI05-200042

This book is dedicated to my wonderful wife and friend, Gloria. I can truly say, I have been in love with the same woman all my life, and if Gloria ever finds out who she is, "Am I in trouble!"

She has put up with my nonsense for over fifty-five years! She laughs at my jokes even if she has heard them over and over. When people ask, "How can you laugh at the same joke so many times?" Gloria always says, "I love his delivery!"

TABLE OF CONTENTS

ACKNOWLEDGMENTS

There are so many people who have told me jokes over the years and added humor to my life, I couldn't possibly put every joke into this first book. That's why there will probably be a second book.

I want to thank the following people who have constantly told me jokes or sent me jokes: My youngest son, Jeff, who sends them to me every day; Alan Rinsler, the "Bionic Man," who has had more body replacements than any person I know; Don Coolidge, who sends me political jokes all slanted toward Republicans because I'm an Independent; Steve and Eve, who are the most consistent with funny stories; Bob Probstle, who always sends me jokes (if you like plain, boring midwestern jokes, they're wonderful), and George Wolfe, another midwesterner who sends me every Jewish joke ever told. And he's not even Jewish.

Bob Schlausen has sent me more jokes and stories than anyone. He sends so much material that he has to use FedEx or carrier pigeons.

My buddy, Don Haselkorn, every once in a while sends me a good joke and if he really likes it, calls me. I always tell jokes to Jack Levine, Rocky Azzarito and Bob Berman, my golf buddies for over twenty-five years. Then Jack retells them but always screws up the punch lines. Bob should just stick to his prune juice.

Rocky does come up with a good joke, once in a while (at his age, it's a great achievement).

Stephen Nichols sends me jokes that drive me up a wall. If he would only include the punch lines, it would really help. Mike Fleishman should stop sending me jokes from afternoon sitcoms because they're not funny! Lenny Frankenthal should stop with the political bullshit and start sending me some funny jokes.

Thanks also to Dr. Don Stein, my brother, who is not funny but who once in a while tells me a good joke. He has written many books on his field of endeavor, brain research. His most recent book is titled, "How to Tell the Difference between a Heart Attack and an Orgasm"—a best seller.

David Nichols, whenever we meet (especially if he's with someone) always says the same thing, "Buddy, tell my friend a joke." Next time he asks, I'll hand them a book and send David the bill.

The following people have contributed to my book with their jokes and funny stories at restaurants, parties, golf courses, public and private toilets, planes, trains, family affairs or just walking along:

Connie Alderman, Bob Kenkel, Sol Fine, Paul Dubrow, Rich Stolls, Arnie Ratner, Dave Stein, Paul Jennings, Phyllis and Bernie Glickstern, Dr. Jeri Nardone, Dr. Mark, Maryann Mitchum, Al Colleta, Martin O'Sullivan, Joel Kurtz, Tom Benson, Larry Schneider, Barry Monheit, Bob Blanford, Tom Benson, Dan Sempert, Al Case, Jim Morgan, Larry Ash, Bob Fitting, Rick Taylor, Rick Wilbur, Sigi Allen, Bill Ihlanfeldt, Peggy Lord Chilton, Elayne Stein, Mel Weiser, Freddy Tunis, Barry Bernstein, Preston Davis, Robert Larsen, David Starkman, Dick Brunning, Dave Feight, Ray Fusco, Mike

LaRusso, Peggy Stanley, Shelly Balick, Joyce Hochberg, Steve Marks, Dennis Kildare, Jerry Kover, and Harvey Lieske.

And to the funniest three guys I have ever known, I'll never forget you: Stan Dubrow, Harry Stern, and Larry Bronson.

Thank you, all!
Buddy

A Special Thanks to Gloria

I decided to write a book on comedy in January, 2004. A lot of people asked me why I decided to write a comedy book at this time of my life. My answer to them is, "At my age, it's now or never."

I had some idea about content, but I just wanted to write it as it flowed from my mind. I know writing consists of a discipline that should be consistent. Unfortunately, I have an attention deficit problem. This creates a small problem when, in the middle of a sentence or idea, I suddenly get up and start washing my car.

At one point, my wife suggested we review some chapters I had written. I sat down to review and immediately decided to polish my golf shoes. I think she finally felt I needed her help when all the pages I had written were spread all over the floor, our bed, and the night stands, and there was nowhere to walk.

Very aware of my frustration, she suggested we pick up all the pages and put them on the dining room table to put them in some kind of order. I gave a sigh of relief at her suggestion.

When she started to review the pages, a look of astonishment came over her face. She read a few of the stories and then she said to me, "This is good stuff, but did anyone ever tell you that you're illiterate?"

I replied, "No one ever called me illiterate. Maybe illegitimate, but never illiterate."

My wife is a college graduate and said, "I don't mean to insult you, but your punctuation and grammar are horrendous."

I said to her, 'Why don't you tell me how you *really* feel about it?"

She said, "You need a lot of help, and if you want me to, I will edit the book for you."

Now I know that you can read the next paragraph, but Gloria says that since her editing, my book is (according to her) easier to read. You tell me if there's any difference.

"I cdnuolt blveiee taht I cluod aulacity uesdnatnrd waht I was rdanieg. The phaonmneal pweor of the hmuan mnid Aoccdrnig to a rscheearch at Cmabrigde Uinervtisy, it deosn't mttaer inwaht oredr the Itteers in a wrod are, the oiny iprmoat-nt tihng is taht the frist and Isat Itteer be in the rghit pclae. The rset can be a taotl mses and you can sitll raed it wouthit a por-belm. Tihs is bcuseae the huamn mnid deos not raed ervey Iteter by istlef, but the wrod as a wlohe."

Amazing, huh? yaeh and I awlyas tought slpeling was ipmorantt!

See! I told you you could read it, but picture my whole book written this way. I think there could be a slight problem!

Anyway, Gloria threw herself into the editing of the book—I mean, like a pit bull attacking a gaggle of geese. The first week, she told me that there were thousands of mistakes. She then laid a real bomb on me. She said, "Buddy, the editing of this book is very difficult. It's going to take me more time than I imagined. I've decided that I want to be paid for my time."

The blood drained from my body. I said, "Get me a hot towel! Listen, sweetheart, I have a better idea."

She said, "What?"

I said, "Well, how about you share in the profits?"

She said, "No way! Just show me the money."

It was difficult negotiating with her, but finally we agreed on a price for her editing. I said, "Now that you've become my editor, will that affect our sex life?"

She replied, "What sex life?"

I must admit, she did a fabulous job. I suggested she might consider going on the road as a stand-up, but that went over like a lead balloon. I have to say that writing this book would have been very difficult without her input. Gloria has been my guiding light and inspiration.

I love her.

Introduction

When my brother Don learned I was writing this book, he asked me, "Who are you writing it for?" My first response was, "Me."

He thought for a minute, and then replied, "So why don't you just print one book?"

After a few seconds, I said, "Well, maybe I want to make some money from it, too."

He said, "Not good enough!" He then posed this question: "If you were on a talk show and the host asked you who this book was written for, think about what you would say."

"OK," I said, "I'm writing for all the people like me who had a dream and for some reason never fulfilled it. Maybe they got stuck in a job that locked them in, or had family responsibilities, or age concerns, or location problems. There are many reasons and they're all valid."

After that conversation with Don, I was even more motivated to write a book. I had never given up on my dream to be an entertainer, and I knew that writing about my experiences would keep them alive for me and for everyone who had believed in me.

Years ago, while I was doing some entertaining on the side, I asked friends to come see my show. A few of them did, and while I was doing my act I asked one of the men in the audience, "How do you like me so far?"

I'll never forget his answer. "Don't give up your day job."

The audience laughed and I did, too. It was a very wise remark. I never did give up my day job, and I turned out to be pretty successful at it. In fact, I went on to become the chairman of a fairly large company. However, my dream of becoming an entertainer was never far from the surface. Somehow, I found ways to fill some of my fantasy and managed to do shows whenever I could.

Sometimes I would do a show in the most unbelievable places, and I'm talking about real joints. Often, I didn't get paid. My personal joke to myself was that if they didn't like me, I'd buy the place and fire everyone.

For years, I kept my dream alive, and finally, when I went into semi-retirement (I don't think I can ever fully retire), I started to live my dreams. Lo and behold, it started happening. Read the book!

The truth is, all things being equal, comfortable surroundings, health, etc., it's never too late. Go for it. Make it happen. If you don't get one hundred percent satisfaction, I'll give you your money back. At least you tried.

Remember, "Don't give up your day job," but for sure, "Don't ever give up your dream."

CHAPTER I

HOW IT ALL STARTED

I remember that when I was about sixteen, I was sitting on the steps of the apartment building where I lived on Bedford Park Boulevard in the Bronx, New York. It was early evening and I was having a very animated talk with my friend, Aaron. We were discussing what we wanted to do when we grew up.

Aaron's brother, Larry Marvin, was beginning to make a name for himself in show business. Show business already seemed to have a hypnotic effect on me, and I fantasized about it all the time—the girls, big cars, and being famous.

A few months later, Aaron invited me to go with him to see Larry when he was asked to fill in for the French singer, Charles Trenet. It was the first time I ever went to a night club, and I was very excited.

Back in the fifties, Trenet was a very popular song stylist. He had been booked into the Embassy Club, a posh venue on 52nd Street in midtown Manhattan, but he suddenly got sick and couldn't perform.

I couldn't wait to see Larry on stage, and Aaron and I got there early. We got lucky and got seated at a table right by the stage. The place started filling up and by show time there wasn't an empty seat in the house.

The orchestra started to play, and the master of ceremonies walked out onto the stage. He was greeted with some mild applause, and he raised his hands to quiet the audience. Everything became very still. Then, he informed the audience that Trenet would not be appearing because of illness. The crowd wasn't thrilled by the announcement, but the emcee quickly told them they were in for a treat.

Tonight, he said, they would see a star being born. If the audience didn't like what they saw, the emcee himself would pay for everyone's drinks! The audience applauded happily, curious to see this hot new performer.

When Larry walked out onto the stage, I couldn't believe how exhilarated I felt. He looked fantastic in his white suit, white shirt and white tie. I remember his opening song was "Rock-a-Bye Your Baby."

When he finished his song, the audience seemed stunned. Then, they broke into the wildest yelling and whistling I'd ever heard. After a few minutes, they got up out of their seats and gave him a standing ovation.

I was sold! I loved the excitement of the show, and the setting truly impressed me. I felt that this was what I was meant to do—entertain! This became a passion that I've carried with me all my life.

Both Aaron and I now knew that we wanted to go into show business and become big stars. I had one big problem. I didn't know what I would do in show business. I told Aaron, "I can't sing, dance or play a musical instrument."

Aaron said, "You've got a big problem."

I said, "What kind of a problem?"

"No talent," he answered.

I told him I had been working on doing impressions of famous actors. Aaron said, "Do an impression for me, but don't tell me who you are impersonating because I want to see if I can guess who it is."

I proceeded to do an impression of Humphrey Bogart. Aaron guessed right away and said, "That's what you'll do, impressions."

So I became an impressionist. I practiced in front of the bathroom mirror. First, I'd light up a cigarette and then, with a very suave look on my face, I'd mimic my favorite actors.

We didn't know at that time that smoking was so dangerous to your health. Later on, health investigators did tests to find out how harmful smoking was to humans. One of the tests they performed was to take a mouse, put a lit cigarette in the mouse's mouth, then lift the tail of the mouse and inhale through the mouse's rectum. If the mouse didn't develop any symptoms, then it was OK to smoke. I think that's how filters were developed.

I worked very hard on my voice to capture the sound and mannerisms of the actors I wanted to imitate. We didn't have television at that time, so I had to go to the movies and sit through the same film several times.

Finally, after months of work, I decided to enter one of the local amateur shows that movie houses used to put on. It was a good gimmick for them. Friends and relatives would come out to catch the performances, and the theaters usually gave out three prizes. The winner got twenty dollars, the second prize was ten dollars and the third prize was five dollars. In those days, this was good money!

I was performing in these shows at least once or twice a week. I usually managed to come out in the top three, not because I was such a great talent, but because most of the other performers were singers and dancers, and there were no other comics.

There was a small theater on Kingsbridge Road in the Bronx called the Windsor Theater. It not only showed movies, but also ran live professional shows on the weekends.

Thursday night was Amateur Night and the winner would get booked for the weekend with the pros. I was obsessed with winning, but for some reason, whenever there was a cowboy singer on the show, I never won. I could never figure out why New Yorkers went crazy over cowboy singers.

Aaron had a devious mind and suggested "stacking" the audience to guarantee my winning the show. I asked him, "How can we do that?"

He answered, "Easy. We persuade forty or fifty of our classmates to come to the show."

I don't know how he did it, but a lot of kids actually showed up. I was really nervous the night of the show. Aaron was backstage with me, and when he saw how nervous I was, he whipped out a flask filled with Southern Comfort and said, "Take a swig, it'll calm you down."

I took a gulp or two and waited for the introduction.

"Here he is, ladies and gentlemen," said the emcee, "from right here in the Bronx—Alan Stewart!" (That was my newly invented stage name.)

My friends all knew me as Buddy Stein, so there was hardly any applause. But when I walked out on the stage, the place went wild. I was so stunned, I almost sobered up. I don't remember what impressions I did, but when they lined up all the contestants, I got the biggest applause. I even beat the cowboy singer!

I did over twelve shows that weekend and I was in heaven. "Show business" was now my life.

I did pretty good impressions of Clark Gable, Cary Grant, Peter Lorre, James Mason, George Sanders, Gary Cooper, and

Walter Brennan, to name a few. The act I did was okay, but my material was pretty bad. Since I couldn't afford to buy jokes, I had to steal them. A lot of comics did that...and they still do.

The place to pick up new routines was in Manhattan, or "Downtown," as the residents of the Bronx called it. If you lived in Brooklyn, you called Manhattan "Uptown." Whatever you called it, Manhattan was the hub of live shows. Every theater between 42nd Street and 50th Street featured a new film and stage show. The live performances were held between the movie showings, so I could see about five shows a day.

I remember the theaters vividly: The Paramount, The Capitol, The Roxy, The Strand, The Old Palace, and Radio City Music Hall, which still presents stage shows. The shows usually featured big bands like Harry James, Tommy and Jimmy Dorsey, Duke Ellington, Count Basie, Stan Kenton, and many others. The shows also featured current star singers like Frank Sinatra, Gordon MacRae, Ella Fitzgerald, and others.

Naturally, my favorites were the comedians or comedy teams. I saw them all—Martin and Lewis, Danny Kaye, Milton Berle, Jack Benny, George Burns and Gracie Allen. There were so many of them and they were all funny.

The price of a theater ticket was twenty-five cents and you could stay as long as you liked. Sometimes I stayed and saw at least three complete shows, including the movies. I tried to write all the punch lines I could remember on the cuffs of the white shirts that I wore to school every day (dressing for school is a lot different today).

I had over fifteen white shirts with punch lines written on the cuffs. My mother was a cleanliness nut. If I got up to go to the bathroom in the middle of the night, my bed was made when I got back.

One day she cleaned my closet, found all the shirts with the writings on the cuffs, and took all my shirts to the Chinese laundry. Three weeks later, "WONG HOW" opened up at the Latin Quarter.

I went on to do many more amateur shows. Finally, like all good things, the amateur circuit ended and the world entered the new era of television. Milton Berle's "Texaco Star Theater" was a smash hit and audiences could see their favorite entertainers on a small screen in the comfort of their homes. Little by little, the Broadway theaters stopped featuring the live stage shows and concentrated on showing new films, instead.

The Ted Mack Original Amateur Hour

The Ted Mack Original Amateur Hour was originally called, *The Major Bowes Original Amateur Hour* and was heard only on radio. In the late '40s, when television was introduced to the public, Ted Mack, who was Major Bowes' assistant, moved it to television. The show used a format still being used today by *American Idol*, where viewers were asked to call in and vote for their favorite performer.

When I was still in high school, I tried out for *The Ted Mack Original Amateur Hour*. I practiced doing impressions of movie stars of that era such as Peter Lorre, Sidney Greenstreet, Clark Gable, James Cagney, Boris Karloff and others.

After my audition, I was told I'd actually be on the show! It was very popular because it was one of the first television shows. It was televised at the old Channel Five studio at Wanamakers Department Store on 8th Street and West Broadway in Manhattan.

There were usually about ten contestants, mostly singers and dancers, along with a cowboy singer. Ted Mack was the host of the show and Dennis James was the announcer. James went on to become quite famous, hosting other shows and announcing for televised wrestling.

There was also a dancer on the show on the commercial. She was enclosed in a large box of Old Gold cigarettes. She had a great pair of legs that would stick out of the box as she danced.

I asked Dennis why they covered up her head and he said she was a two-bagger. I didn't know what that meant but he thought it was hilarious. He told me she was so ugly that anyone who went out with her had to wear a bag over his head, too.

The night of the performance was really scary. It was the first time that I would be seen on television. At that time, no one knew how much of an audience we would have. We didn't even know how many people owned television sets.

I was the only comedy relief on the show and I was very nervous. Dennis James introduced me. He announced, "Ladies and gentlemen, let's give a warm welcome to Alan Stewart," (I'd chosen Alan Stewart as my stage name) "who is appearing here for the first time."

Ted Mack always interviewed the talent for a few minutes before they began their acts. He asked, "So, you are Alan Stewart and you are going to do impressions for us. Have you appeared anywhere locally as an amateur?"

I answered, "Yes, sir, I've appeared at some small hotels in the Catskill Mountains."

He then asked, "Can you tell us a little about yourself? Remember, this is a family show."

I talked a little about my show business aspirations. He then asked me if I'd always wanted to be an impressionist.

I answered, "Actually, I wanted to be a tap dancer but I had a hernia operation recently and couldn't dance, so I became an impressionist."

Ted Mack said he was sure that the audience would like to see a few steps. I stood up, grabbed my crotch and proceeded to do some dancing. The audience went crazy and I thought Ted Mack would have a heart attack! Dennis James couldn't stop laughing!

I then proceeded to do my impressions. I ended my act as Walter Brennan impersonating Abe Lincoln doing the Gettysburg Address. I waved a small American flag just before the end of the Address. The audience gave me a standing ovation. I went over so well that I appeared five more times. I felt fantastic about those appearances.

The Catskills

The Catskill Mountains were a two-hour drive going north from Manhattan. There were over 300 hotels and bungalow colonies in the area. It was now 1949 and I had just turned eighteen. Larry Marvin had a gig that weekend at a hotel called, Sha-wan-ga Lodge. He asked me and Aaron to go with him and I felt great. Sha-wan-ga was known as a real swinging place.

We left early in the morning in Larry's new blue Caddy convertible. It was a beauty with white leather seats. We had a lot of laughs driving to the hotel. Larry was starting to drink liquor excessively. He began the morning drive with a couple of belts from a flask. He was drinking Southern Comfort and it had a kick like a mule.

On the way to the hotel, the conversation got around to girls. Since I didn't have much experience, the thought of being with girls was the most important thing on my mind. Larry and his brother were very tall and handsome and the girls flocked to them. Aaron said to Larry, "Gee, with all the chicks you have, you are so selfish...you never share them with us."

Larry thought for a few minutes and said, "OK, I'll tell you what I'm gonna do for you guys. Tonight after the show, go up to my room, wait about twenty minutes, then get undressed. Take a bottle of Southern Comfort with you and hide in the closet. I'll bring a girl up to the room and when I start to sing, 'Take Me In Your Arms,' you'll rush out of the closet and you can have a good time with her."

That night after Larry's show, the girls came flocking around him. They didn't even notice Aaron or me. We all had a few drinks. Then, finally, Larry gave us the high sign to leave. We went up to his room with great expectations.

After being in the room for a while, we took off our clothes, got into the closet and waited. We waited for what seemed like hours. I asked Aaron if he thought this plan would work. He said, "Sure, no problem."

Finally, we heard the door to the room open and heard Larry's voice. I whispered to Aaron, "When do you think we should come out of the closet?"

Aaron reminded me, "As soon as Larry starts to sing 'Take Me In your Arms,' we step out of the closet."

We were in the closet for over thirty minutes, totally naked and bombed out of our skulls. Finally, the big moment came. I took a deep breath, threw the closet door open and we stepped out. I threw out my arms and yelled, "Taa daa!" when it caught it my throat.

Sitting on the bed were fifteen men and women. They started to laugh and applaud! We were in shock and I didn't know what to do. I said the first thing that came into my mind. "If you don't pay your milk bill, I'm gonna piss in your bottle."

Everyone roared with laughter. Aaron and I ran back into the closet to thunderous applause and wouldn't come out 'til everyone in the room left. I told Aaron, "That was very funny," but he wasn't too happy.

He said, "When I see Larry, I'm gonna punch him in the mouth, that son of a bitch!"

We got dressed and left the room. Aaron wanted to go back to the city and told Larry we were leaving. But I told Aaron, "We can't leave. We're in the middle of nowhere, we have no money and there are no buses running."

Then Larry saw us, came over with a big smile on his face and slapped me on the back. He said this had been the best practical joke he had ever pulled.

Larry agreed to drive back to the city that night. He collected his music and we went out to the car. The hotel was on the side of a small mountain and the parking lot was on the edge of a cliff.

We got into the car. It was very late at night and we were all still tipsy. Larry started the car and put the top down. Then, Aaron said to him, "You're a real ass for making fools of us."

Larry said, "It was just a joke, so why are you getting so mad?" This was the wrong thing to say because Aaron hauled off and hit Larry on the side of his head.

I was in the back seat and soon they were throwing punches at each other. Meanwhile, the car started rolling toward the edge of the cliff. When I saw this, I started to scream, "We're going over the edge. Stop fighting and stop the friggin' car!"

No answer—they were still throwing punches.

I said to myself, "I'm out of here," and leapt out of the back seat. Aaron saw me and yelled, "Holy shit, stop the car!" At the last minute, Larry stepped on the brake not more than a foot from the edge.

Aaron wanted to continue the fight, but I grabbed him and said, “Enough, let’s go home. Someday, we’re going to remember this night and laugh about it.”

I don’t know about Aaron, but as for me, I’ll never forget it.

Doorway To Fame

Doorway to Fame was the name of a new television show that was based on the *Ted Mack Original Amateur Hour*. After my appearance, it was lovingly called, “Doorway to Shame.”

At the time, big names in show business were reluctant to appear on television. It wasn’t a proven commodity and no one wanted to take the first step. Then, *The Texaco Star Theatre* with Milton Berle came on the air.

Auditions were being held for the *Doorway to Fame* show at the Old Romanian Night Club on 48th Street and Broadway in Manhattan. I went there to try out for the show and met George Scheck, the producer of the show. I did my impressions and he liked them, so I made the cut.

The show was being done at the new CBS television studios on 50th Street and 10th Avenue. It was very exciting for me. Since I’d been on the Ted Mack show a few times, I had a little experience in how television worked.

When I got there, I went into the makeup room and people started to work on me. They loaded me up with face makeup and eyebrow liner. I was so tan, it looked like I’d just gotten back from Miami Beach.

The master of ceremonies was a fellow named Red Benson. He was very charming and bubbly. Finally, the show was about ready to go on. The musicians were lined up and preparing to start. Benson said, “Alan, you’re on first. You have six minutes and not a second longer.”

“Wait a minute,” I said. “I didn’t even rehearse with the band yet!”

He said, “Don’t worry about that. They’ll follow every move you make. We want this to look unrehearsed.” He continued, “This is live TV, and besides that, you are going to be the very first act seen in Chicago via coaxial cable.”

I found out later that this show was a trial run for the cable people. They were more interested in seeing if the cable worked than in how the performers did.

Well, I went on! The first thing I remember saying was how happy I was to be on the first coaxial cable television show and that we were broadcasting live from New York City. The second thing I said was, “The difference between radio and television is, on television you can see where the smell is coming from.”

This freaked out the producers. The stage spots were so bright that the heat actually melted the makeup on my face. I felt as if my lower lip could touch my belly button. One guy said that I looked like Rubber Man. It was just another experience for me on my way to stardom. Ha!

Red Benson told me later that my image came over very well and that the Chicago viewers were very happy with the results of the cable experiment. I was still a senior in high school when George Scheck asked me to come and work for him in his new production company after I graduated.

“Thanks,” I told him, “but I really want to be an entertainer.” I was too young to understand what a great offer he was making me. His production company went on to great success. He produced a talent show called, *The Star Time Kids* and he also managed Connie Francis and Bobby Darin, as well as a lot of the talent who performed on his show.

Prom Night...With Jackie Gleason

Larry Marvin was booked into the Riviera nightclub, situated on the cliffs of the New Jersey Palisades overlooking the Hudson River and the George Washington Bridge. At that time, the Riviera was one of most prestigious nightclubs in the country. It held 1,500 people and had fabulous views.

Larry was co-starred with Jackie Gleason, who went on to become famous with *The Honeymooners*. It was the night of my senior prom, as well as the opening night of the show. We booked a table for eighteen people. All the guys wore white dinner jackets and the girls wore evening gowns. We all looked pretty good. We had dinner, a few drinks and everyone was feeling great.

The lights went down and the band played a big fanfare. Bill Miller owned the club and was also Larry's personal manager. There were booking agents and managers from all over the country in the audience.

Larry did a great show and the audience gave him a standing ovation. At that time, the emcee was supposed to introduce Jackie Gleason, but Larry had other ideas and held onto the mike. He was really stoned.

Standing there, looking down at the audience, he said, "I have a surprise for you! We have a new young star in the audience who will be appearing with George Sanders and Gene Tierney in a new movie. This young man, besides being an accomplished actor, is also a fabulous impersonator."

By this time I was beginning to get a weird feeling, my heart started pumping wildly, and my mouth went completely dry.

Larry went on, "It's my pleasure to introduce this young star. Let's give a warm welcome to Alan Stewart."

At this, I almost threw up and said, "What the f-k. Is he crazy?" Aaron pulled me out of my chair and pushed me toward the stage. I thought I would die, but I went up on the stage.

The band gave me a downbeat and Larry said, "Kill 'em, kid...."

I went onstage and did a few impressions and the audience applauded warmly. I walked off the stage to all the fanfare and felt pretty good.

Meanwhile, Jackie Gleason was flipping out. He grabbed a guitar and ran after Larry screaming, "You had no right to bring on that kid." When he saw me, he said, "Get out of my way, you bastard, I have a show to do!" Bill Miller also blasted Larry for bringing me on!

That night, I enjoyed performing so much, I knew show business was in my future. The performers' guild, A.G.V.A., fined Larry for his actions and shortly afterward, Bill Miller dissolved his contract with Larry. It's too bad that such a great talent became lost to alcohol.

And They Said It Would Never Last

A bolt of lightning hit me! Actually it was Cupid's arrow! I spotted a girl at a dance in Poe Park, a local park in the Bronx named after Edgar Allen Poe.

Every Friday evening during the summer, dances were held in the park. Big bands were hired to perform in the band stand. The park was always packed with teenagers having a great time.

I usually went to Poe Park on Friday night to attend the dance, and it was there I first saw Gloria, standing near the bandstand talking to a few girls. She was as pretty as a picture and still is! She lived on Long Island, another suburb of New York, and was visiting her old friends.

My heart started beating very fast as I approached her and I said, "How about a dance?" She looked at me, put out her arm to me and that was it! I was smitten. She felt the same about me.

We talked a little as we danced to the great sounds of the music of the '40s. We just seemed to be on the same wavelength. I joked with her and she laughed. We really enjoyed being together on that summer night in the park, with the great music playing. It seemed like heaven to me!

After that we went out on dates several times a week for a while, and since we lived so far away from each other, I had to do a lot of traveling. So we decided we wanted to get married. That was actually the only way to get out of your house in those days. Our friends said it would never last, but they were wrong! We did get married and it has lasted fifty-five years and still counting!

Down By The Riverside

The late 1950s were a special time in my life. I was twenty-seven, and Gloria and I already had two sons and were looking for a nice camp to send the boys to for the summer. Sleepaway camps were very expensive and we heard of a small hotel in the Catskills called the Riverside. It was located at Divine Corners, a small hamlet about ten miles from Loch Sheldrake. It wasn't a town, just a larger hamlet.

The Riverside offered a full day camp for our sons for the entire summer, three meals a day, activities, and shows. It was situated in a lovely mountain area. I spent two weeks there on my vacation plus weekends.

We performed in a lot of the amateur productions, and I acted as master of ceremonies for the professional shows that were brought in on the weekends. We had a great time there, and many of our friends came up to the hotel and loved the place, so they stayed on, too.

Charlie Rapp was one of the booking agents. He worked out a contract for the entertainers, promising them a flat fee of $20,000 for the summer. He booked them into the 300 hotels and bungalow colonies, and most of the acts jumped at the contract. Charlie booked them for three shows a night and some big name acts would work the smallest of places, like the Riverside.

Some of these entertainers were Morey Amsterdam, Henny Youngman, Jack Carter and more. These professionals were not thrilled to be working in such small places, but since they signed the package, they had no choice but to work where Charlie sent them.

One night, I met another guest by the name of Arnie Rattner. I thought he was a real nut case and I was right. He went onstage that night and did a bit that Sid Caesar had made famous. It was the "fighter pilot" routine.

This was a very funny pantomime of an American fighter pilot during World War II who's being attacked by a squadron of ten German aircraft. He proceeds to evade and then shoot down all ten of his attackers.

What made this routine so funny was that Arnie did a great impression of the famous comedian, Sid Caesar, who originally did the routine. He included all the sound effects: diving and turning, machine guns blazing, rockets going off. You had to be there to appreciate Arnie's sound effects and motions—he was simply hilarious, and the hit of the show.

I was so impressed, I asked Arnie if he was interested in forming a comedy team with me. He jumped at the idea and we agreed we would meet after the summer and start working on an act.

Before I tell you about me and Arnie, I want to share one experience that stands out in my mind at the Riverside. One weekend, they held a masquerade party. Every guest had to dress up, or they wouldn't be allowed in the dining room for dinner. To take away a meal from that group would be tantamount to a personal disaster.

There was a good joke going around at the time, and since Gloria and I had invited ten people up that weekend, we agreed we would reenact the joke and dress accordingly for the masquerade.

This was the joke: A guy gets up in the morning and is late for work. He dresses very quickly and doesn't even eat his breakfast. He starts to run out of the house to go to work, and just as he reaches the door, his wife yells out, "Honey! When you come home tonight, don't forget to bring home six black chickens."

He says, "OK," and leaves for work. He finishes work at 6 p.m. and phones his wife to make sure he would bring home the right thing. He says to his wife, "Did I hear you correctly? Did you want me to bring home six black chickens?"

She says, "That's right."

He asks her, "Why in hell would you want me to bring home six black chickens?"

She says, "To act as pallbearers for the dead cock you brought home last night!"

The women who acted as the six black chicken-pallbearers were all dressed in black. I was wrapped in Saran wrap (to simulate the dead cock), and placed on a stretcher. They carried me into the dining room followed by all the wives dressed in black, crying and moaning. As we reached the long table where our friends were seated, the pallbearers were to lift up the stretcher and slide me on the table.

Unfortunately, they lifted it too high in the back and very low in front, so as they tipped the stretcher, I slid onto the floor under the table. It was a wild scene, never to be forgotten. There were roars of laughter. Our group won first prize that night which included an extra plate of chopped liver and heartburn for the rest of the evening.

Chapter 2

EARLY BOOKINGS

The Casa Calabria

As I mentioned before, I got together with Arnie Rattner, the guy who did Sid Caesar's fighter pilot routine at the Riverside. We met in the Bronx in early September and started working on material for our comedy team.

We decided not to use Rattner as a stage name because Rattner and Stein was a little too Jewish. We felt we should have a better name that would work and be a little more "American." So we came up with the name "Rogers and Stein."

The first line we used in our new routine was, "The name of our team is Rogers and Stein, but we left out the hammer." Otherwise people would think we were the great Broadway song and lyric writers of that time, Rogers and Hammerstein. We worked very hard to develop material for our act and it took us over a year to finally feel ready to do a show.

Arnie's mother-in-law worked for the Metropolitan Opera at the time. She was the wardrobe lady and fitted all the costumes for the cast of the opera. Arnie asked her if we could get two outfits, preferably Russian Cossack uniforms. Lo and behold, she came through. They were incredible outfits.

We had black pants with high black leather boots, red jackets with bright gold buttons, and a bandolier of bullets (I think that's what it was called). The outfits also came with a large Cossack hat that was cone-shaped and made out of black Persian lamb. She also gave us long beards and mustaches. I didn't know if we looked comical, bizarre, or just like two nut cases.

We worked very hard on our act and I was able to get us a booking at the Casa Calabria, an Italian men's club in New Rochelle, New York. They had functions two or three times a year. We were booked into their clubhouse, and I was able to get the grand sum of fifty dollars for the two of us.

We had never worked together in front of an audience before so I was very nervous. Arnie was in his own world—nothing seemed to bother him.

The night of the show we packed up our costumes and I took along a small flask of Scotch that I kept nipping at for at least two hours before the show. By show time, I was totally wasted.

There was a crowd of about 150 people at the club, and it was a very happy and loud crowd, drinking their *vino* and whatever else was available. The lights dimmed and the emcee came out onto the floor under a spotlight.

He said, "Tonight, I'm proud to introduce a new comedy team doing their first professional performance at our club. Now, without further ado, let's have a big Italian welcome for the comedy team of Rogers and Stein!"

For our opening, we had rehearsed with a piano player. Now, he started playing a Russian Cossack melody. You must picture this: I was totally out of it and Arnie didn't have to have a drink because he was *always* out of it.

I had developed a couple of dance steps to bring us onstage. We started singing at the top of our lungs, "Usa-seta-bella-ninka, usa-seta-bella-thinka, la la la la la la la, Khrushchev is a dirty stinker!" We were spinning around the dance floor like two lunatics.

As I kept turning and spinning, I started getting dizzy, and on one of my spins I leaped into the air and went flying headlong into a table, smashing into a plate of spaghetti. Wine glasses went flying, pasta was thrown about like confetti. Women started screaming, but the piano player kept playing. I managed to right myself, with tomato and meat sauce flowing down the front of my jacket.

There was an incredible uproar and people were shouting, "Kill the bastards!" In all of the turmoil, Arnie and I just barely escaped with our lives. We never used our Russian Cossack opening ever again, but we never gave up!

Arnie and I formed a professional relationship that would last for over ten years. We were living in our own fantasy world and had professional pictures taken and musical arrangements done. We even had special teal blue tuxedos designed for us. I always remarked to Arnie, "We may not be good, but we look great!" In our hearts we believed we would be stars.

Every time after that fiasco that we did a show that wasn't too good, I would work on changing our act. You can imagine how many times the act was changed. It was a lot of fun, though, and it kept us feeling that we were part of the show business scene.

Callback

Callback is a term in show business meaning that if after your first audition they think you have some potential, you'll be called back so the powers that be can take another look. In this case, it was the name of a pilot for a CBS television show.

The idea was to perform without an audience. However, the producers proposed that the audience at home should act like a studio audience and phone in their reactions.

The team of "Rogers and Stein" was picked to be the comedy relief on the show. It was being televised in color (one of the first shows during that time) and Arnie and I were really excited about doing this show.

We even hired a comedy writer from the J*ohnny Carson/Tonight Show* to write a six-minute routine for us. It was the first time we had invested in any type of material. I don't recall the writer's name but I do remember how much he wanted to do the bit: $1,500.

When he told us the price, Arnie went into shock and I needed hot towels to calm me down. I said to the writer, "What if it bombs?"

He said, "That's the chance you have to take."

I said, "What if we give you half up front and the balance after the show?"

He said, "It doesn't work that way. You pay up front; otherwise, don't waste my time."

I think Arnie and I had been offered four hundred dollars for both of us to do the show. I asked the writer, "Can we at least get an idea about what the routine will be?"

He told us, "The idea takes place in a baseball stadium. Buddy plays the manager of the ball team. Arnie is the pitcher. Arnie's first part is done in pantomime. He gives up three home runs in the first inning.

"Buddy, you come out to the pitcher's mound and ask him for the baseball as you call for a relief pitcher. Arnie doesn't want to give you the ball. You become very angry and insist on getting the ball. You tell Arnie that it doesn't look nice that he won't give you the ball.

"Finally, Arnie relents, but instead of handing you the ball he throws it at you. Now you get angry and tell him to pick up the ball and hand it to you like a gentleman and so on. What do you think?"

We both liked the bit and decided to buy it. Well, they televised the show on an afternoon. It was a little difficult working without an audience to play to, but at least we got a few laughs from the cameramen.

The show was going to run a few weeks after it was televised. We were given the dates, and we sent cards to every person we could think of, including every agent in the phone book.

Now, remember the premise of this show. The home viewers, according to the producers of the show, would laugh in the privacy of their homes.Then they would be instructed to call the station and vote on the contestants. I never found what the winners would receive.

The day of the showing, my living room was packed to capacity with friends, relatives, and strangers. Even our mailman was there!

When Arnie and I came out, my living room burst into applause. It was the first time I had ever seen myself in color. We looked pretty good. We started to do our fifteen-hundred-dollar baseball bit, and most of our friends said they liked it. But I didn't hear any roars of laughter.

I said, "How come you didn't laugh?"

My friends said they felt a little funny sitting there in the dark with everyone, and I guess no one wanted to be the first to start laughing.

Well, that was the first and last show for Callback. It was never seen or heard of again. The experiment had failed but at least we got a pretty good routine out of it.

We added the routine to our act and it always got a mild reaction, but at least it was an original routine. It was also the last time we ever bought a comedy bit. We found that it was more convenient to lift or "steal" material as needed for our routines.

The Moulin Rouge

This was one of the first club dates that our manager, Larry Fallon, got us. It was out on Staten Island, a bit of a trip from the Bronx. I wouldn't say the place was run down, but they had to paint it before they could condemn it.

The dressing room was so small that once you went into the room, you couldn't change your mind. If you turned too quickly, your ass got stuck on the doorknob.

We had to share our dressing room with another act on the bill, but we didn't mind because she was a gorgeous young stripper who was making her debut. She was from Texas, and to her, Staten Island seemed like "the big time."

When she entered the room, we introduced ourselves. To say the least, she was not the swiftest kid on the block. She began to get undressed as if we weren't in the same room. It took us by surprise and made our small dressing room very, very steamy.

She then took off her bra. Her boobs stood out like beacons! Arnie let out a large gasp and asked her, "Are they real?"

She replied, "I just had a new procedure called implanting, and this will be the first time I expose them to my audience."

Arnie was fascinated. "Do you have any feeling in them? They look so tight!"

She replied, "I don't know. I'm the only one who's ever touched them."

"Would it be all right if I touch them?" asked Arnie.

"OK," she said.

Arnie proceeded to squeeze and fondle her breasts. "So, do you feel anything?" he asked.

She said, "Well, I'm getting a warm feeling."

By this time, there was a dense fog in the dressing room.

Arnie then asked, "Would it be out of line if I kissed them?"

I couldn't believe what I was hearing and seeing! She started to moan a little as Arnie kissed her breasts. At this point, they didn't even know I was in the room with them.

Then she said, "Is there anything else I can do for you?"

Arnie paused, looked at her with his big, hound dog eyes, and said to her, "Maybe you have some cookies?"

It was the biggest laugh I had all night.

The Hawaiian Cottage

Some of the places we worked in bring back the memories even after so many years. Our manager booked us into the Hawaiian Cottage in Cherry Hill, just outside of Philadelphia. We told Larry we didn't want to travel out of the New York vicinity but he begged us to do the gig because we would have a lot of exposure and it would open up a lot of doors for us.

Both Arnie and I had full-time jobs. I was trimming windows and Arnie also had a steady job. It was a difficult decision to make because we would have to work six nights of the week.

What Larry failed to tell us was that it would be seven nights a week and we would have to do three shows a night. It was late June and the weather was extremely hot. I had to finish up my day job, meet Arnie and drive ninety miles to Cherry Hill.

The first night we got there was a real shocker. We had never worked at a place as big as this. They had a huge poster with our picture at the main entrance. It was very impressive and kind of scary.

The Cottage was huge, holding over fifteen hundred people in the main room. It also had at least three other halls for different affairs that would be going on throughout the night.

When we arrived, we were taken to meet the head man. His name was Joe something, but looking back, his name could easily have been Joe Soprano. He said, "How ya doin?"

We answered, "Pretty good!"

He said, "OK, this is your schedule. First, youse rehearse with the band. We gave you a nice dressing room because youse guys are the stars. Youse work the main room first, then the ballroom, then the Cottage Room. It's a seven-night contract and youse better be good!"

"Hold it!" I said. "First of all, we were told it was a six-night booking."

Joe became very agitated. "I don't give a f—k what you were told. Your manager signed a contract for seven nights and you better do it. You get the meaning?"

Arnie and I looked at each other and said, "You're the boss!"

We were taken to our dressing room, and it was pretty nice. In fact it was the best dressing room we had ever been in. In the past, most of our dressing rooms couldn't be compared to a regular dressing room. Often, we had to hang our clothes from a metal pipe in the basement, next to a boiler. Sometimes, we'd even been told to use the men's room to change in. I really hated that.

Our dressing room at the Hawaiian Cottage had makeup mirrors with stage lights, which made us feel very professional, and the room was very spacious. It was a far cry from hanging our clothes from a metal pipe.

Unfortunately, it was summer, and there was no air conditioning and no fan, and Arnie and I were really sweating.

I said to Arnie, "This is crazy, how can we put on our makeup? You know, we don't need this. This really sucks—no air conditioning, no fan, and Fallon lied to us. He said we would work only six nights, and now it's seven. It's bullshit!"

Arnie immediately said, "Let's leave!"

But I reminded him, "We can't just walk out. If we do, we will never be able to work clubs again and besides I don't think these guys would hesitate to break our legs. However, we don't have to work under these conditions. Let's go see Joe and tell him we won't work unless we get a fan."

We walked out of our dressing room and met the dance team who were on the bill with us. We introduced ourselves and told them we were going to Joe's office to get a fan.

They laughed and said, "You gotta be kidding, you'll never get satisfaction. We were here last year at this time and it also was hot as hell. We told them we needed a fan and Joe told us to get lost if we didn't like it! Well, we have no choice. We need the money!"

I said to Arnie, "Arnie, we can't work under these conditions. We tell him we either get a fan or we're out of here!"

I also told Arnie that I would do the talking. So we went over to the "den of evil," and I must say I was more than a little nervous. On the way, I told Arnie, "This may be our last appearance in show business."

We got to Joe's office and there was a real goon blocking the way. He said, "Yo! Whatta youse want?"

I said, "We have to see Joe."

He replied, "He's busy, get lost!"

I said, "Oh, yeah? You better tell him unless he sees us we're splitting."

He said, "Youse gotta be kidding. He sure ain't gonna be happy!" Then he went into Joe's office and came out a few seconds later and said, "OK, he'll see ya."

We walked in to Joe's beautiful, air-conditioned office. Boy, what a contrast to ours! He looked at us and said, "Make it short, I'm busy."

I replied, "OK. It's too fucking hot in our dressing room. We either get a fan or we're leaving."

He looked at us without speaking, then said, "You're crazy. You're gonna walk out on me? We're sold out tonight! You walk and you're out of the business."

I said, "We don't care, we're not gonna subject ourselves to this heat because you're too cheap to give us a fan!"

I honestly don't know where I got the nerve, but I went on. "You've got twenty minutes, then we're packing and leaving."

We turned and left the office. I looked back at Joe, whose mouth was open. I think he was in shock. I said to Arnie, "I'm sure an entertainer never spoke to him like that."

Arnie said, "Wow, you really told him off."

"We shouldn't have bought the new tuxedos. Oh, and remind me, when we see Larry Fallon, to tell him to kiss our asses," I replied.

We started to pack and were getting ready to leave when there was a knock at the door. I opened it and standing there were two of Joe's goons with a twenty-four-inch standing fan.

I said, "Hi, come in, guys. You can put the fan in that corner."

They did it and left without saying a word. The dance team followed them in and said, "We can't believe it. You really got a fan!"

I said, "Well, I guess you gotta make a stand against these assholes."

They said, "We could never do that, we need the bread!"

I said, "I understand. And by the way, if you want to change into your costumes in here, you're more than welcome to do so."

We rehearsed with the band and it was very exciting. The band was in a pit and then on cue, the stage would rise like an elevator. It was a fairly big group, probably at least twenty pieces and very impressive.

That first night was really something. I opened the show as the master of ceremonies. The first thing I talked about was the management and how cheap they were. I told the audience how hot our dressing room was and that we had no air conditioning.

I told them when I got here I weighed at least one hundred pounds more and as far as money, management was so tight, we'd get paid off in pineapples. It got a big laugh!

We never did so many shows. The first night we did at least five shows. We went from hall to hall. There were weddings, Bar Mitzvahs, business meetings, etc.

I only stopped between shows to go to the bathroom. There were about ten guys in the bathroom, so I even did twenty minutes of comedy there. The second night, Joe wanted to see us in his office before the shows. When we walked in, he was all smiles.

He said, "You know, youse guys are really something. I like ya. In fact, I want ya to stay another week and I'll double your salary. You know, youse got real balls coming in here and threatening me. But I like that and youse guys are pretty funny. In fact, because of youse, I'm gonna put fans in all the dressing rooms! So whatta you say, do we have a deal?"

Well, we begged off, telling him that we had bookings that week and couldn't do it. It was a great experience, but driving back and forth to Long Island every night was wearing us out. We never got home before 2 a.m. and I had to be up by 7 a.m. to go to work.

My wife was really pissed off and said, "You're a nut case and you better start thinking about what you want—a shoe business or show business."

I wasn't really in the shoe business. My main source of income was window trimming, and most of the stores I trimmed were shoe stores. I actually trimmed windows from 1952 to 1972, when I sold my business and took a position with Trimco, a distributor and manufacturer of store displays.

During those twenty years, I did as many shows as I could.

I must tell you about one incident that related to both shoe and show business. Arnie and I were set to audition for a new TV pilot. The day of our audition, I had been booked to do a window display for a shoe store in Yonkers, New York. Our audition was set for 11 a.m. that same morning.

I got to the store at about 8 a.m. and started to lay out the displays. My assistant, Steve Walker, knew about the audition, but I had told him not to tell the store owner why I had to leave early. Instead, I concocted a story about going to Manhattan to pick up some material I'd forgotten for the display.

Lenny, the owner, flipped out when I told him I needed to leave for about an hour or so. He said, "How can you leave me with all the shoes from the windows spread all over the store? I won't have any place for the customers to sit."

I apologized profusely. He finally said, "You better get back here soon, or I'm firing you."

I promised, leaving Steve to make any further excuses he could think of. Jumping into my car, I started driving at breakneck speed, weaving in and out of traffic. I had to change into a tuxedo for the show, so I stopped in a secluded area of Van Cortland Park, a huge park in the north Bronx.

I got out of my car and started strippping off my work clothes, standing in my underwear. It was late November, and I was freezing my butt off as I started to put on my tuxedo shirt.

Suddenly, a police car pulled up behind me and two big cops got out. In the typical language of the New York police, one of them said, "What the f—k are you doing here?"

I said, "You won't believe me, officer, but I'm on the way to the city for an audition and I have to wear the tuxedo for the show."

The other cop said, "I know this is a very simple question, but why the f—k didn't you get dressed at home?"

Meanwhile, I'm standing there freezing while trying to explain the situation. Why I didn't have a breakdown at that time was probably because I was already a mental case.

I finally convinced the cops to let me go. I got to Manhattan, did the show and rushed back to the park, where I changed my clothes, got back to the store and finished decorating the windows. I arrived back home and collapsed from exhaustion.

This story has a happy ending. We did get chosen to do the first show! (See "Callback").

The Merv Griffin Show

I don't recall how we signed up with our personal manager, Larry Fallon. He was the best we could get, considering all the restrictions we put on him as far as getting us show dates, but he was weak in getting us bookings. The restrictions were that we would not travel out of state. We wouldn't work for less than a hundred and fifty per booking and he had to give us at least two weeks notice before we started a gig. Usually an agent or manager would throw you out in the street if you came up with those kinds of restrictions, but the Fallon Theatrical Agency was no William Morris Agency.

I felt that Arnie and I were ready to expand a little, so I asked Fallon to try and get us some television work. He laughed and told me we would have to be a more established act before he would even try to get us on TV. I was a little perturbed by his answer. I told him if he couldn't get us on television, I would.

I proceeded to call some of the television stations to see what we would have to do to get booked on a show. The television show directors all told me that to get on a variety show, our manager should contact the talent coordinators on any show. They were the people who decided whether you would get on a show. I informed our manager and he still felt it was a waste of time.

The first TV show I called was *The Merv Griffin Show*. When the operator answered the phone, I told her I was the manager of a new comedy team from the West Coast. I also told her that the team was on tour and would be in New York City for only a short period of time. She was very gracious and put me through to the show's talent coordinator, whose name was Dick Carson.

I asked her if he was any relation to Johnny Carson. She laughed and said, "He's Johnny's brother." I could never figure how Dick Carson was working for Merv Griffin while his brother was Griffin's biggest competition for late night audiences.

Anyway, Dick picked up the phone and was very pleasant. I repeated the same story I gave the operator, telling him my name was Alan Stewart and I represented the great new funny comedy team of *Rogers and Stein.*

We talked for a short while and he suggested that the team come in to speak with him. We set up a date for our meeting. I was very excited and immediately called Larry and Arnie. They both freaked out. I told them that I used my old stage name of Alan Stewart and posed as the team's manager. Fallon said he wanted to go to our meeting with Dick Carson, but I told him, "You can't go."

We never had a lot of confidence in Fallon—not that he didn't try. But his vision wasn't our vision. Fallon booked us in every little joint from Sal's Pizza Kitchen to the Luxor Baths, anywhere to keep us working. I had a feeling I could handle the interview better without him there, but Fallon was very upset until I told him he would still get his commission.

The day of the meeting arrived and Arnie and I were very, very excited. This could be our shot at the big time. We started fantasizing about how we would make it big and become stars.

We finally arrived at the studios (I think it was WNBT) and were escorted into Dick Carson's office. The office really stunned me because it was the smallest office I had ever been in. There was a desk and chair for Dick, but only one chair for a client.

We talked for a few minutes and Dick asked where our manager was. I told him he was called out of town on some urgent business. He then asked what our act was about. After I went over our routines, he told us that we would only do six minutes and it had to be clean material. He then wanted to see a couple of minutes of our act.

I told him, "Do you really think were gonna get up and audition for you under these conditions? We're pros! Would you like us to do three minutes on your desk?"

He said, "You know something, Buddy, you're right. I like your attitude." Then he took out his calendar and gave us a show date. I wanted to leap over the desk and kiss him. We left the office on a cloud.

As I recall, we only had a couple of weeks to prepare our six-minute debut. We called and notified every agent we ever knew to give them the date of our show. I was told to contact the show's office to receive any last-minute instructions. They informed me that there would be only one other guest on the show with us and they expected the biggest viewing audience they ever had. The guest would be Bob Hope.

I couldn't believe it! I talked with Arnie and we went into overdrive getting ready for the show. We bought new tuxedos and had our hair styled. I figured with all those people watching us, we had to look good.

The night of the show we arrived very early for makeup and instructions. We were given a very nice dressing room and everyone was wonderful to us. Dick Carson came to see us and said if we didn't do well, his ass would be in a sling.

I told him not to worry, that we were totally prepared. Bob Hope went on first. We never got to meet him. Arthur Treacher, who was Merv's Ed McMahon, came into our dressing room to see how we were doing. Arnie was eating some dessert that was supplied by the show and was completely nonchalant. I had a couple of drinks and actually felt ready to go.

Onstage, Bob Hope started talking and never stopped. By the time we were supposed to go on, the show was over and time had run out. The producer felt very bad but he gave us another date a week later. We started all over again notifying all our relatives, friends, agents, etc.

We even got paid for the show we didn't do. Larry Fallon was happy that he was going to be paid twice for the same show but it was a very nervous week for me because I still had my job to do and had a family to support.

The following week, we arrived at the studio all hyped up for the show. The makeup people went to work on us and Arthur Treacher, who had taken a liking to Arnie, came to our dressing room to tell us who would be appearing on the show with us.

The first guest was Hayley Mills, a young starlet at the time. I think she was only eighteen years old and had appeared in many films. She was the daughter of the famous British actor and producer John Mills.

The second guest was June Havoc, the actress and sister of Gypsy Rose Lee. The last guest was Richard Pryor. This was his first late night appearance, and of course he went on to become a top standup comic and a movie star.

After we were made up, we were moved to the green room, where all the guest entertainers assembled. The green room was set up so you could watch the guests on a television screen and be ready to go out on stage. Arnie and I were very hyped up and nervous.

Arthur Treacher told us that we would be playing to over six million viewers, but not to think about that. He said, "The most important thing is to get the studio audience to like you." He continued to tell us, "Don't play to the cameras, just work the studio audience."

I was still hyperventilating when we were introduced by Merv. We ran out on the stage and launched ourselves into our routine. When we were rehearsing for the show, we decided since this was our first major break, we would cram as much material as we could into the six minutes we'd been given.

We did everything! We did impressions, singing, comedy routines and monologues. The audience didn't have the chance to laugh before we were doing another routine. It was crazy, like doing the Minute Waltz in twenty seconds.

The audience gave us a fairly good reception, and Merv was, to say the least, a bit stunned. After the applause subsided he looked at us and said, "I've been in this business a long time and believe me I have never seen anyone do an hour's worth of material in six minutes."

The audience started laughing as Merv kept shaking his head in wonderment. As we left the stage, he called out and said, "You guys should try to slow it down just a wee bit."

So that was our shot at fame. Who knows what would have happened if we had just done one of our routines, rather than trying to cram our whole act into six minutes. I think the overall reaction from our friends was simply, "WOW!"

We did get some mileage out of doing *The Merv Griffin Show*. Larry Fallon got us some more club dates, and after that we sort of wound down our careers in show business. Arnie went back to selling injection molded plastics and I continued trimming windows.

I also wrote a screenplay based on our experiences. It was called *Don't Give Up Your Day Job* and was the story of two guys with families who tried to make it in show business.

The San Su San

This story is one of the highlights of my short show business career. The comedy team of Rogers and Stein was getting some serious bookings. We were booked into The San Su San nightclub in Jericho, Long Island, New York.

This club was usually a stepping stone to the famous Copacabana nightclub in New York City. Most of the big-name acts appeared at the San Su San prior to opening up at the Copa.

We had appeared earlier in the year with a pretty popular male singer, Lou Monte, whose claim to fame was that he owned the musical rights to "Mala Femina," a well known Italian song that many other artists recorded. Every time it was played, Lou Monte got royalties. He told us that he became very rich just from that one song.

We did quite well working a week with Lou, and because of that, King Broder, the L.I. theatrical agent, booked us to work with Jerry Vale. He called me at home to tell me of the great shot this would be for the team because Jerry Vale was a big recording star and had a very large following on Long Island.

I don't recall what we got paid for the week, but it wasn't much. He also said to me that we would open the show for Jerry and that we should limit our time onstage to six minutes.

I told him he was nuts. It took us six minutes just to walk out on the stage. He said, "If you want the gig, do six minutes!"

I was very upset with having only six minutes to do our act. I called the owner of the San Su San and told him of my conversation with King Broder. His name was Tony something, or Philly or Angie. I always had a problem remembering first and last names.

He told me, "King Broder can go to hell! Do as long as you want, I'm paying you, not him." Like he was paying big money for us!

The opening show was on Mother's Day, and the club had three shows scheduled—a two o'clock show, a six o'clock dinner show and a nine o'clock late show. All three shows were completely sold out, and had lines around the block.

Arnie said to me, "I never knew we were so popular."

"They're here to see Jerry Vale, not us," I said, setting him straight. He really believed people were coming to see us.

Before the first show, Tony or Angie or Philly came to our dressing room. He wanted to wish us good luck and also told us there was a very important man who would be at the opening show. He told us he'd be sitting at the table off stage on the left side, and if we did any schtick with the audience, to be sure not to go near his table.

We met with Jerry Vale before the show and asked him (just as a courtesy, since he was the star of the show) if he would mind if we opened with a song. He not only told us to do whatever we wanted, but offered us his musical director to conduct for us.

That was great. There were at least twenty musicians in the orchestra, and they took up most of the stage. That gave us about two feet to work in, but it was great working with such a talented bunch of musicians.

Before we went out on stage, I reminded Arnie not to fool around with the table on our left. I didn't want to end up as part of the foundation of a new building.

He said, "No problem!" As soon as we were introduced, Arnie ran off the stage to the table on the left. There were three guys sitting there who looked like part of the cast from the Sopranos.

Arnie said something to one of the men, who started to reach into his suit pocket. I felt sure that we were going to get shot. I could even see the headline: "Rogers and Stein Die at the San Su San Nightclub."

Arnie went on to try one of his tricks that never worked, pulling the tablecloth off the table with all the dishes and glasses. The idea was that the cloth would come off but the dishes and glasses would remain on the table. I saw the trick done by a magician once, and it was great. Unfortunately, Arnie never mastered it.

Tonight, when he tried it, everything went on the floor. The Godfather never blinked, but the audience went wild with laughter. Then, we proceeded to do one of the funniest shows we had ever done. People either loved us or hated us. There was never a feeling that we were okay or not bad. We either were lousy or we were wonderful.

When we got back to our dressing room we were elated, but the feeling didn't last long. Two of the guys that had been sitting with the Godfather were waiting for us!

I whispered to Arnie, "Let's go down fighting."

Then, one of them said "Yo! Youse guys were very funny and Mr. Bonnanno wants to share a drink with you after the show. Be there!"

Then they left.

"Wow!" I said to Arnie. "We are really lucky they didn't break our legs. Why did you try to do the tablecloth bit? It never works."

He said, "I forgot which side the table was on that we weren't supposed to fool around with. Who knew it was Joe Bonnanno's?"

We started to put on our regular street clothes (we always wore tuxedos when we did shows) when there was a knock on the door. A man entered, and said, "Hi, I'm Mort Farber, Jerry Vale's personal manager and also the lawyer for the Copa. You guys did very well today."

I said, "Gee, thanks, Mort."

He then said something that really floored us. "How would you like to open for Jerry at the Copa in two weeks?"

After I caught my breath, I said, "Well, I think we have to speak to our manager to see if we're free at that time."

He said "OK, get back to me tomorrow and I'll set up an appointment for you to meet Jules Podell, the owner of the Copa."

He then told us why he was in a hurry. Jerry was scheduled to open with Allan and Rossi, a big time comedy team, but they'd had a fight and broken up. So they couldn't fulfill their commitment. That's why he had to know ASAP, so he could get an opening act for Jerry. I remember Mort was a very nice guy.

Arnie and I had always talked about the moment we would get a break. Now it was decision time. My fantasy was becoming a reality. What would I do? I was married, with three sons and a wife I loved. How could I go full time into show business?

Oops! I forgot to mention that Mort Farber also told us that if we did well at the Copa, he'd sign us for forty weeks to open for Jerry around the country.

It was a major decision and I needed time to think about it. I was going crazy as to what I should do. I called Mort Farber to set up a date at the Copa to discuss what direction we would take and whether we would open for Jerry Vale or not.

I called Arnie to see what our options were. He said to me, "Whatever you decide is fine with me." Arnie never made a decision, and I always felt that if we went into the business full time, I'd end up killing him.

I once asked him, "What would you do if I decided we should jump off the Empire State Building?" He said if we held hands he would jump.

We met with Mort Farber and Jules Podell of the Copa. Our manager, Larry Fallon, was also present. I think Rodney Dangerfield's manager was there, too.

Mort said, "Here's the deal, you do well at the Copa and I sign you to work with Jerry for forty weeks." I don't remember how much he offered us, but it wasn't significant. It was actually less than I was earning trimming windows.

I said, "It's a wonderful opportunity you're offering us, but for me to keep up my current responsibilities, I have to decline."

Larry, our manager, couldn't believe my response. He started yelling at me and said, "How could you refuse this offer? This could make you stars! I worked like a dog to get you guys this far. You can't turn it down."

I said, "Listen, Larry, you didn't even know we were booked at the San Su San until I called you. I just can't do it. I can't leave my wife with all the responsibilities of taking care of two teenagers and a baby. I agonized over this decision and it's a done deal."

They all looked at Arnie. He looked back at them without saying a word. Finally, Mort Farber said to him, "How do you feel about it, Arnie?"

He slowly looked around for a few seconds, and then very softly said, "If Buddy holds my hand, I'll jump."

I guess that was our big chance. Who knows what would have happened if we'd taken the offer. That ended my fantasy about being a big star. The idea of becoming stand-up comics had been a lot of fun and gave us a release from our everyday normal lifestyle. However, I never regretted the decision not to pursue the fantasy. I really don't think Arnie and I would have stayed together for any length of time. He, too, had family situations that came into play.

It's been years since I heard from him but there has always been a warm spot in my heart for him. I'll always remember him fondly and our partnership.

PS: I forgot to mention after the first show at the San Su San, we sat down for a drink with Joe Bonnanno. He told us that he really enjoyed our performance and it got him very nervous when Arnie pulled the tablecloth off the table. He said with a smile that he'd love it if Arnie and I would take a ride with him! We graciously refused!!

CHAPTER 3

THE CELEBRITY CONNECTION

Danny Thomas

Danny Thomas was born Muzyad Yahkoob in Lebanon in 1914. When he started to do comedy professionally, he changed his name to Amos Jacob, then later changed it to Danny Thomas. He was a fine actor, comedian and producer. He also received the Congressional Medal of Honor for all his charity work to help the underprivileged. Larry Gelbart, who wrote for The New York Times, said that Danny could take a short story and make it long!

The following story that Danny told is one of my favorites:

This guy was driving his car in a very rural area, late at night. He suddenly realized that his tire was flat. He stopped his car on this deserted country road. He got out of his car, opened the trunk and took out the spare tire. He looked for the jack so he could jack up the car to change the tire. He searched throughout the trunk but could not find the jack. He was upset, but then he remembered passing a farmhouse a little way back. He decided to walk back to the farmhouse to get help.

It was a very dark night and as he walked, he started talking to himself. He said, "What if the farmer doesn't have a jack? Then I'm in real trouble! Ah, he's got to have a jack. What if no one's at home? Ah, someone's got to be home! What if he has a jack and won't loan it to me? Well, I could offer him some money. What if he doesn't take the money? Well, when I explain the situation, he'll take the money and lend me the jack.

"But then again, he could be a real creep and just tell me that he doesn't care what my problem is and he won't give me the jack. Some people can be real mean...I may have to beg him for it!"

Finally, very agitated, he sees the light from the farmhouse. As he approaches the house, he continues to talk to himself. "I don't believe that this guy won't lend me his jack. Here I'm stranded and he won't help me out!"

He steps up to the front door and rings the bell. After a few moments, the door opens and a little old man in his pajamas says to him, "Can I help you?"

"Yeah, you can help me! You wanna know how you can help me? I'll tell you how you can help me. Take your jack and shove it up your ass!!!"

Myron Cohen

Myron Cohen was a great storyteller during the '50s and '60s, at the height of Ed Sullivan's TV show, *Toast of The Town*. Myron appeared often on the show and was a big hit with his stories of Jewish humor. Before becoming a comedian, he had worked in Manhattan's garment center. His fellow workers were so impressed with his great storytelling abilities, they encouraged him to go into show business. He did and became a very popular comedian in that era.

I was a young man when I met him. He was starring at a nightclub in Manhattan, the Old Romanian, on Broadway and 48th Street. They served excellent food and had some decent entertainers performing there.

My friend, Larry Marvin, was co-starring on the bill with Myron and invited me to the show on opening night.

Myron was standing at the bar. I was about eighteen years old then, so I stepped up to the bar next to him. He was very cordial and offered me a drink. I told him that I admired the way he told such humorous stories. He thanked me and then I said to him, "I remember when your act died in Freeport, Long Island."

He looked at me for a few moments and then said, "I never did a show in Freeport, Long Island."

I said, "I know! I did your act and it bombed!"

Actually, I never did. But the words just came out of my mouth, probably because of the two beers I'd just had!

He laughed and thought that was very funny. Later on, during his show, he talked about what I'd said and it got a good laugh!

Here are some of Myron Cohen's stories:

The Loan

Sam goes up to his friend, Joe, and says, "Lemme have twenty dollars."

Joe says, "Here's ten dollars."

Sam looks at the money and says, "I asked you for twenty."

Joe says, "I know, but this way, you lose ten and I lose ten!"

The Two Partners

(told with a Yiddish accent)

Two partners mafe a fortune in the dress business. They decide they really want to do something different. Sam says to Morris, "You know, for a few dollars, the Russians are sending people to da moon."

Morris says, "Dat's different, all right. Call the Russian Embassy and find out when the next space capsule is leaving!"

So Sam calls the Russian Consul and asks when the next capsule is leaving for the moon. He adds, "And how much vill it cost?"

The Russian tells him the cost is ten million dollars a person to go to the moon. Sam says, "Vell, everyone goes to the moon, so ve vant to go to da sun."

The Russian says, "If you get within one million miles of the sun, the spacecraft will burn up and you will be killed immediately."

Sam thinks for a minute and then says, "Vell.. ve'll go at night!"

Caught In the Act

(also told with a Yiddish Accent)

Jake is talking to his best friend. He says, "Vot a story, I got to tell you. I vas in bed with Sadie Greenbaum, ve t'ought her husband vas out of town. Ve heard the key in the lock. So Sadie yells, 'Sam is home, so qvick, get out the vinda!'"

His friend says, "Vot did you do?"

"Vell, vat could I do? I leap out of da bed, open the vinda, climb out and I'm holding on to the vinda sill vit mine fingers!" says Jake.

"So den, vot happened?" questions the friend.

Jake says, "He spots me and takes his penknife and sticks it under mine fingernail!"

The friend says, "Dat must haf made you mad."

Jake continues, "No, dat didn't make me mad. Den he pours molasses all over me, tears open a pillow case and dumps the feathers on me. I luked like a tchicken!"

The friend says, "Dat must haf made you mad!"

Jake says, "No, I vasn't even mad den. Vot got me mad vas ven I luked down. I vas only one foot off the ground! Dat got me mad!"

Abe and Becky

Abe and Becky are working their way up the social ladder. They are invited to their neighbor's upscale party, where the subject for the evening is famous poets, writers, and composers. The group is in a discussion after dinner, talking about famous composers like Puccini, Mendellsohn and Browning.

Then, one of the guests brings up Mozart. Becky says, "I know Mozart. I was just with him yesterday on the number five bus to the beach."

The guests are dumbfounded by her statement but continue talking like nothing was said. On the way home, Abe says to her, "How can you say something like that? You don't know how to keep your mouth shut. You're also stupid! You know that the number five bus doesn't go to the beach!!"

The Pool

A wealthy garment manufacturer invites a group of people to his Long Island estate for the weekend. When they all arrive, he takes them on a tour of his grounds. First they walk past the gardens, then past the tennis courts and then to the swimming pool area. To everyone's astonishment there are three pools.

One of the guests says, "How come you have three pools?"

The owner replies, "Well, the one on the left is for people who like warm water, and the pool on the right is filled with cold water."

The guest then says, "What about the third pool, it's empty?" The manufacturer says, "That pool is for my friends who don't like to swim!!"

Rodney Dangerfield

At least 40 years ago, I was entertainment chairman for my Masonic Lodge in New York City. One of my duties was to hire entertainment for our yearly dinner dance.

A friend of mine said he knew of a comic who would be happy at the chance to work. He connected me to Rodney, who had just changed his stage name from Jack Roy. So I hired him at a minimum price. I probably booked him for two hundred dollars for his one-hour appearance. No one at the time had ever heard of him.

I asked Rodney how he wanted to be introduced. He said to me, "Just bring me on, kid, and I'll handle it."

So I announced, "Ladies and gentlemen, here's Rodney Dangerfield." Rodney then proceeded to do about forty minutes, but the only one laughing was me. After he finished his bit, he walked off to very tepid applause.

Actually, he bombed! The Masons and their wives came over to me, complaining how bad he was and how could I hire such a bum! All I heard for two weeks were complaints about what a stiff Rodney Dangerfield was.

Several weeks later, I turned on the *Ed Sullivan Show* on a Sunday night and who was appearing? Rodney! He was fantastic. Sullivan had him back many, many times, and of course the rest is history. Every time I saw some of my fellow Masons, I never hesitated to remind them that they had no taste.

As Sullivan would say, "Tonight, right here on this stage, right here in front of you is a very funny guy, Rodney Dangerfield!" Today, the world is a lot less funny: Rodney Dangerfield has left us. In celebration of his life, here are some jokes he enjoyed telling:

> It's been a rough day. ...I got up this morning, put my shirt on, and the button fell off.
>
> I picked up my attache case, the handle fell off.
>
> Now, I'm afraid to go to the bathroom!!!

> I was kidnapped when I was a kid.
>
> The kidnappers sent a piece of my finger to my parents. But my father said he wanted more proof!!!

> I was making love to a girl and told her, "You're so flat-chested." She said, "Get off my back."

I was so poor when I was a kid that, when I grew up and went to an orgy, it was to eat the grapes!!!

———

The first time I had sex, I was afraid!! After all, I was alone!!

———

During sex, my wife likes to talk to me. The other night she called me from the Hilton!!!

———

What do I know about sex? I'm a married man!!!

———

If it weren't for pickpockets, I'd have no sex life at all!!!

———

I got a call from my girlfriend the other night. She said, "Come on over, there's no one here."

I went over...and there was no one there!!!

———

Last week I told my psychiatrist, "I keep thinking about suicide." He said, "From now on, you pay in advance."

Don Rickles

I first saw Don Rickles many years ago at a small nightclub called the Valley Stream Park Inn in Valley Stream, New

York. I was completely awed by his rapid-fire delivery and his caustic sense of humor.

I remember saying to my wife, "This guy will either be a big star or someone will kill him."

I did not personally witness the following stories, but they were told to me by people who are very honest. I recall hearing the second story from Tom Poston, the actor/comedian, at a golf outing at Mountain Gate Country Club in Los Angeles.

Rickles was the opening act for Frank Sinatra at the old Sands Hotel in Las Vegas. It was his first appearance with Sinatra and his first shot at the big time. After Don's great performance, Frank told him after the show that he thought his act was terrific.

Rickles then asked Frank if he would do him a favor. Rickles had made a date with a very beautiful young lady and had to meet her at a bar later that evening. He asked Frank (since he was such a big star), if he wouldn't mind stopping by the bar to say hello to him and the girl. Rickles said it would really make a tremendous impression on her, and make it easier for him to make out with her.

Sinatra agreed and said to Don, "I'll drop by later and we'll have some fun!"

Sure enough, later that evening Rickles was sitting at the bar with the young lady having some cocktails when Sinatra made his appearance. When he walked into the lounge bar, everyone in the place started to applaud.

Sinatra proceeded to walk over to Rickles as planned. He patted Rickles on the back and said, "Hi, Don, that was a great show you did tonight and it's a pleasure being on the same bill with you."

Picture this: Rickles slowly turned to Frank and in his most Don Rickles delivery replied to Sinatra, "Listen, kid, I told you at least a hundred times, don't bother me when I'm with someone. Now take a hike. Can't you see I'm busy?"

Sinatra just walked away, shaking his head.

The other story about Don Rickles really cracked me up. This was later on in his career, when he was a big attraction. He was appearing in Las Vegas as the headliner. The show was packed and Don had just started his performance. If you have ever seen him in person, you know he'll criticize anyone at any time during his act.

It seems three men of Arab nationality came into the room wearing their traditional head dress and proceeded to sit down at one of the tables close to the stage.

Rickles noticed them and stopped what he was saying. He then announced, "Ladies and gentlemen, this could happen only in our great country. Here I am, a Jewish performer working with a Protestant musical director, in front of a great stage band conducted by a Catholic, and who walks in but three Arab gentlemen. (This was during the time of turmoil in the Middle East. As long as I can remember there have always been big problems in that area.)

Rickles then said to the audience, "To show we have no hard feelings, let's give these three guys a big American welcome." As the audience started to applaud and whistle, the three Arabs were a little confused and were hesitant to stand up to acknowledge the reception.

Rickles yelled out, "C'mon guys, stand up and take a bow. We're all friends here."

So the three Arabs cautiously stood up. They finally get to a full standing position and started to wave to the crowd.

Rickles then yelled out, "Open fire!"

Buddy Hackett and the K-Swiss Corporation

I was working on some promotional projects for the K-Swiss Shoe Corporation back in 1990. I'd been asked to assist in interviewing people for a video production, a "man in the street" type of program, that the company wanted to use for their national sales meeting that year.

We had an entourage of four people, a video photographer and a very loose script. Our first stop was at the Beverly Center Mall in Beverly Hills, Los Angeles. I was feeling quite excited about the video production. Armed with a portable mike system, I positioned myself and the crew at the bottom of a very high escalator that carried people out to the street.

My simple question was, "What do you think K-Swiss is?"

I got some unbelievable answers: "It's a chocolate bar; it's something to do with the Swiss olympic team; it's a travel agency. ..."

An old man said, "The Swiss should have done more to help the Jews during World War II. Will this interview be on television and how much will I get paid?"

We assumed from these interviews that K-Swiss was not very well known at the time and that more promotional advertising had to be done to make "K-Swiss" a more familiar name as a major shoe company.

After we traveled around Los Angeles for a while, we decided to go to a private tennis and golf club called Mountain Gate Country Club. I am an avid tennis player and the crew wanted to get some videos of me playing tennis at the club, wearing the K-Swiss Classic tennis shoes.

I glanced up as we parked our cars in the parking lot and noticed Buddy Hackett, the comedian. I had met Buddy a few times prior to this, as we were both members of this country club.

He had not shaved, looked really grubby and his clothes looked as if they'd come from the Salvation Army.

I said, "Hi! Buddy!"

His lip curled as he looked at me and he said, "How ya doin?" Two of the girls from the crew came over and I introduced them to Buddy. I told Buddy we were doing a "man on the street" interview video and asked if he'd mind being interviewed.

I also told him we had a very low budget and couldn't pay him a fee for his appearance.

Buddy said, "Sure, but I want the girls with me in the video."

"No problem," I said, and we started filming as he held the girls around their waists. I started the interview with, "Hi, we're here at the Mountain Gate Country Club on the hills overlooking the San Diego Freeway and we're going to interview the famous comedian, Buddy Hackett."

Then, switching to my interview patter, I said, "So, Buddy, what do you think of K-Swiss?"

He turned around with the girls on either side of him, dropped his pants, bent over and mooned us.

As we gasped, he turned his head toward us and said, "You want me in this video? You pay, otherwise you get my ass!" He then pulled up his pants and left.

We were all stunned! I never did find out if they used that scene when the video was presented at the sales meeting!

We had many club tournaments during the year. There were many celebrities who were members of the club due to its location in Beverly Hills.

At one post-tournament luncheon, Tom Poston was asked to get up and entertain with a few jokes or stories. He graciously agreed to tell some stories about his show business experiences.

Among them was this story about Buddy Hackett. Before Buddy became a comedian, he worked as a rookie policeman in Fort Lee, New Jersey. He was out on patrol one night and came to a deserted parking lot. He noticed a convertible car parked with its top down.

He parked his police car a few feet from the other car, took his flashlight, got out of the car and walked over to the parked car. He shined his flashlight on the car and noticed there was a couple making out in the back seat of the car. The guy was eating this girl up! The girl jumped up and screamed, and the guy turned and pulled up his pants.

Buddy said, "Making out in a public place is against the law. Let me see your license!"

The guy said he didn't have his license with him. Buddy looked at him and then said, "Do you have a Diner's Club card?"

CHAPTER 4

DOCTOR JOKES

There are thousands of jokes about doctors. Here are some of my favorites:

Most doctors ask you to set up an appointment six months in advance. How do you know when you're going to be sick? I went to my doctor recently, complaining about a pain in my back.

My doctor asked, "Have you ever had this pain before?"

I told him that I did. He said, "Well, you got it again!"

I also told him I had a ringing in my ears.

He said, "Don't answer it!"

Then I told him that I couldn't hear very well.

He said, "You're much better off, the way things are today!"

Medicine is a great profession. The doctor gets a woman to take off her clothes and then he sends her husband the bill!

My friend was very sick and the doctor gave him only six months to live. My friend then told his doctor he couldn't pay his bill, so the doctor gave him another six months!

My doctor believes in shock treatments—his bill!

I told my doctor that I had groin pain. He examined me and said my muscles were strained. He asked me how many times a week I made love.

I told him, "I make love every Monday, Wednesday and Saturday."

He said that I would have to cut out Wednesday.

I told him, "I can't do that, Doc. That's the only night I'm home!"

I know a doctor who charges $200 a visit, and if you're sick he charges more!

I knew a young nun who had hiccups constantly. Her mother superior made an appointment for her to see a doctor and went with her. After her examination, the young nun ran out of the office crying.

The mother superior said, 'Why are you crying?"

The young nun said, "The doctor told me that I was pregnant."

The mother superior stormed back into the doctor's office and said, "How dare you tell the young nun that she was pregnant?"

The doctor said, "Got rid of her hiccups, didn't it!"

Every Jewish mother wants her son to be a doctor. If he's half retarded, a lawyer. If he has no brain, an accountant. (Jackie Mason)

A woman goes to her doctor for an examination. She comes home and her husband says, "So what did the doctor say?"

She answers, "He said that I have the body of a thirty-year-old."

The husband says, "What did he say about your sixty-year-old ass?"

She smiled and said, "We didn't discuss you!"

This guy was sitting in the doctor's office. He was moaning, complaining that everything hurt him. "No matter where I touch, I have pain!"

Finally, the doctor calls him into the exam room. About twenty minutes later the man came out and I said to him, "So what did the doctor say?"

He answered, "He said my finger's broken!"

A Chance Meeting

A doctor is walking down Main Street. He sees one of his elderly patients in the middle of the street, fondling, grabbing, squeezing this young woman. The doctor walks over to him and says, "Henry, what are you doing?"

Henry says, "Hi, doc! Well, you told me in the office I should get a hot momma and feel cheerful."

The doctor replies, "I didn't say that! I said you have a heart murmur! Be careful!"

Never Tick Off A Nurse

A big-shot attorney had to spend a couple of days in a hospital. He was a pain to the nurses because he bossed them around. None of the hospital staff wanted anything to do with him. The head nurse was the only one who stood up to him. She came into his room and announced, "I have to take your temperature."

After complaining for several minutes, he opened his mouth. The nurse said, "I'm sorry, but I can't use an oral thermometer today."

After more complaints, he rolled over and bared his behind. After the nurse inserted the thermometer, she said, "I have to get something. Now just stay like that until I get back."

She left the door open on her way out. He cursed under his breath as he heard people laughing, as they were walking past his door.

After a half hour, the man's doctor comes into the room.

"What's going on here?" asked the doctor.

Angrily, the man answers, "What's the matter, Doc? Haven't you ever seen someone having their temperature taken?"

After a pause, the doctor confesses, "Not with a carnation."

Embarrassed

A man is lying in the hospital with an oxygen mask over his mouth. A young nurse is sponging his hands and feet. The man mumbles from behind the mask, "Are my testicles black?"

The young nurse replies, "I'm only here to wash your hands and feet."

He struggles again to ask, "Nurse, are my testicles black?"

Finally, she pulls back the covers, raises his gown, holds his penis in one hand and his testicles in the other to take a closer look and says, "There's nothing wrong with them!"

The man pulls off his oxygen mask and replies. "That was very nice but...are...my...test...results...back?"

The Witch Doctor

(The punchline has to be done with a Yiddish accent)

This takes place in deepest, darkest Africa! There's a circle of savages and the drums are beating at a frenzied pace.The natives are all chanting. In the center of the circle is a large fire.

All of a sudden, a man leaps out into the center of the circle. He has a bone through his nose, bones hanging from his ears, and his body is painted in wild colors! He's chanting and jumping. The drums are beating wildly! He dances near the fire. Then he throws some powder into the flames. The flames explode! The savages are getting wild.

One old native women turns to another old woman sitting beside her and proudly says, "Dat's my son, the doctor!"

The Wrong Prescription

A woman went to her doctor for a follow-up visit, after the doctor had prescribed testosterone for her. She was worried about some of the side effects she was experiencing.

"Doctor, the male hormones you've been giving me have really helped, but I'm afraid that you're giving me too much. I've started growing hair in places I've never had hair before."

The doctor reassured her, "A little hair growth is a perfectly normal side effect of testosterone. Just where has this hair appeared?"

She answered, "On my balls."

Urine Analysis

I went into the hospital for a complete check up. They assigned a nurse to me who's gotta be a real sadist. Every two hours during the night, she wakes me up for a urine specimen. When I finish, she hands me a glass of apple juice. I hate apple juice.

After being woken up for the fourth time, I had it with this Nazi. I went into the bathroom and took one of the glasses of apple juice, told her it was a specimen and gave it to her. She looked at it and said, "My, this looks very cloudy."

I said, "Let me see that." Then I took the glass and drank from it.

She screamed, "What are you doing?"

I told her, "I'm running it through my system again to see if it clears up." (Alan King)

An Out-of-Body Experience

This woman is having an out-of-body experience. She's standing in front of God and asks him, "How long do I have to live?" He looks at her and in a godly voice says, "YOU HAVE FIFTY MORE YEARS."

She wakes up in the morning and rushes to her plastic surgeons. They flatten her belly, raise her boobs, do nips and tucks all over her. When she's healed, she gets dressed, runs out of the hospital, gets hit by a milk truck and is killed.

She goes to Heaven and says, "God, how could you do this to me? You promised me I had fifty more years."

And God says, "I didn't recognize you."

The Big Decision

An old guy can't get an erection so he goes to the doctor. The doctor says, "I can help you. For $25,000, we can make you very active."

The old man says, "That sounds good, but I would like to discuss it with my wife."

The doctor says, "No problem, when you reach a decision, call me."

The old guy goes home, talks it over with his wife and calls the doctor the next day. The doctor says, "So, did you come to a decision?"

The old guy says, "Yeah, Doc, we made a decision— We're gonna redo the kitchen."

The Prognosis

This older couple goes to their doctor for the husband's yearly visit. After the doctor examines him, he says to the husband, "Mike, would you please step out for a few minutes, I'd like to discuss some things with Beverly."

So Mike goes out and Beverly says, "What's the problem with Mike?"

The doc answers, "Well, he's not doing too well, but there's nothing to be alarmed about, Bev. If you make him four good meals a week and have sex with him at least three times a week, he should be fine in a short time."

Bev goes out to the waiting room. Mike says, "So what did the doctor say?"

Bev replies, "He said you're gonna die!"

The Annual Checkup

I went to the doctor for my yearly checkup. The doctor said, "You're in great shape. How old are you? Sixty-nine? Wonderful! When did your father die?"

I said, "Who said he died?"

The doc said, "Really? How old is he?"

I said, "He's Ninety-three."

The doc said, "You're gonna live a long life! When did your grandfather die?"

I said, "Who said he died?"

The doc said, "This is amazing. How old is he?"

I told him, "He's 120 and that's not all. He's getting married next week."

The doc said, "Why would he want to get married at his age?"

I said, "Who says he wants to get married? He has to!"

The Permit

A man walks into his doctor's office. The doctor says, "How can I help you?"

The man says, "I eat like a horse!"

The doctor says, "A lot of people eat like a horse. Just cut down on the portions you eat."

The man says, "Doc, you don't understand. I eat like a real horse. I eat hay, oats and barley."

The doctor takes out a pad and starts writing.

The man asks, "Are you writing me a prescription?"

The doctor replies, "No, I'm writing you a permit to shit in the street!"

Sperm Count

An eighty-year-old man went to his doctor's office to get a sperm count. The doctor gave the man a jar and said, "Take this jar home and bring back a semen sample in the jar tomorrow."

The next day, the eighty-year-old man reappeared at the doctor's office and returned the jar, which was still empty.

The doctor asked what happened and the man explained, "Well, first I tried with my right hand, but nothing. Then, I tried with my left hand. ...Still nothing. My wife tried with her mouth, first with her teeth in, then with her teeth out, and still nothing. We called the lady next door and she tried to help, too, first with both hands and then even trying squeezing it between her knees. But still nothing."

The doctor was shocked. He said, "You asked your neighbor?"

The old man replied, "Yep...and no matter what we tried, we couldn't get the jar open."

The Gynecologist

A woman went to her gynecologist and upon lying on the table with her legs up in the stirrups, the doctor examined her and commented, "What a large vagina you have."

Upon which the lady said, "Well, you didn't have to say it twice."

And the doctor replied, "I didn't!"

A Grandmother's Story

A sweet grandmother telephoned Mount Sinai Hospital. She timidly asked, "Is it possible to speak to someone who can tell me how a patient is doing?"

The operator said "I'll be glad to help, Dear. What's the name and room number?"

The grandmother in her weak, tremulous voice said, “Holly Finkel in Room 302.”

The operator replied, “Let me check. Oh, good news. Her records say that Holly is doing very well. Her blood pressure is fine; her blood work just came back as normal, and her physician, Dr. Cohen, has scheduled her to be discharged Tuesday.”

The grandmother said, “Thank you. That’s wonderful! I was so worried! God bless you for the good news.”

The operator replied, “You’re more than welcome. Is Holly your daughter?”

The grandmother said, “No, I’m Holly Finkel in Room 302. No one tells me shit.”

The Dentist

A dentist noticed that his next patient, a little old lady, was nervous, so he decided to tell her a little joke as he put on his gloves. “Do you know how they make these gloves?” he asked

“No, I don’t,” she replied nervously.

“Well,” he spoofed, “there’s a building in Mexico with a big tank of latex and workers of all hand sizes walk up to the tank, dip in their hands, let them dry, then peel off the gloves and throw them into boxes of the right size.”

She didn’t crack a smile.

“Oh, well, I tried,” he thought.

But five minutes later, during a delicate part of the procedure, she burst out laughing.

“What’s so funny?” he asked.

“I was just envisioning how condoms are made!”

Gotta watch those little old ladies!

The Phone Call

A distraught senior citizen phoned her doctor's office. "Is it true?" she wanted to know, "that I have to take that medication you prescribed for the rest of my life?"

"Yes, I'm afraid so," the doctor told her.

There was a moment of silence before the senior lady replied, "I'm wondering, then, just how serious my condition is because this prescription is marked 'NO REFILLS.'"

Labor Pains

A married couple went to the hospital to have their baby delivered. Upon their arrival, the doctor said he had invented a new machine that would transfer a portion of the mother's labor pain to the baby's father.

He asked if they were willing to try it out. They were both very much in favor of it.

The doctor set the pain transfer to ten percent for starters, explaining that even ten percent was probably more pain than the father had ever experienced before. However, as the labor progressed, the husband felt fine and asked the doctor to go ahead and kick it up a notch.

The doctor then adjusted the machine to twenty percent pain transfer. The husband was still feeling fine. The doctor checked the husband's blood pressure and was amazed at how well he was doing.

At this point, they decided to try for fifty percent. The husband continued to feel quite well. Since the pain transfer was obviously helping out the wife considerably, the husband encouraged the doctor to transfer ALL the pain to him.

The wife delivered a healthy baby with virtually no pain. She and her husband were ecstatic.

When they got home, the mailman was dead on the porch.

———

Change of Heart

This guy has a huge member and he talks in a very high voice. His family and friends are always ridiculing him. Finally he goes to the doctor. After examining him, the doctor says "I can help you, but it would mean taking off at least six inches of your penis."

The guy says, "Would that give me a deeper voice?"

The doctor says, "Absolutely!" So, it's done.

About six months later, the guy has a change of mind because he doesn't like his lower voice. So he goes back to the doctor and tells him, "I want my penis restored to its original size."

The doctor looks at him and says in a very high voice, "A deal is a deal!"

———

Another Checkup Story

During her annual checkup, a gorgeous young woman was asked to undress. She said to the doctor, "I'm embarrassed to take my clothes off in front of you."

The doctor said he fully understood and closed the lights.

She said, "Okay." When she finished undressing, she asked the doctor, "What should I do with my clothes?"

The doctor said, "Just put them on the chair on top of mine."

CHAPTER 5

SENIOR MOMENTS

Anyone can get old.

All you have to do is live long enough!

Groucho Marx

Here are some special favorites of mine about a condition we'll all get to experience—if we're lucky!

The Dentist

An old man walks into a dentist's office with a toothache. After the dentist examines him, he says, "That tooth has to come out. I'm going to give you a shot of Novocaine, and I'll be back in a few minutes."

The man grabs the dentist's arm and says, "No way. I hate needles and I'm not taking a shot."

So the dentist says, "Okay, we'll go with gas."

The man replies, "Absolutely not. It makes me sick for a couple of days. I'm not having gas."

So the dentist steps out and comes back with a glass of water. "Here," he says. "Take this pill."

The man asks, "What is it?"

The doc replies, "Viagra." The man looks surprised and says, "Will that kill the pain?"

"No," replies the dentist, "but it will give you something to hang on to while I pull your tooth."

The Will

An elderly woman from Brooklyn decided to prepare her will and make her final requests to her rabbi. First, she wanted to be cremated, and second, she wanted her ashes to be scattered over Bloomingdales.

"Bloomingdales!" the rabbi exclaimed. "Why Bloomingdales?"

The woman said, "Then I'll be sure that my daughters visit me twice a week!"

Honeymoon

A 103-year-old man marries a forty-nine-year-old woman. On the night of their honeymoon, he says, "Would you mind if I slip into something comfortable?"

She says, "Of course not."

So he slipped into a coma!

Living In Sin

An old man goes into a church. He says, "I want to see a priest."

The priest comes out and says, "Can I help you, sir?"

The old man says, "Yes, Father. I will be eighty-five on my next birthday and I'm living in sin with a thirty-five-year-old woman. Every day I fool around with her—I grab her, squeeze her, whatever I want!"

The priest says, "Listen, my son, it's wonderful that you will be eighty-five years old on your next birthday. Don't worry about anything. Put a donation on the plate, do a novena, and pray with your beads."

The old man says, "But I'm not Catholic, Father!"

So the priest says, "Then why are you telling me all this?"

The old man says, "I'm telling everyone!"

Old Friends

Two old guys meet on a street. The first guy says, "Joe, how've you been? I haven't seen you in years. Boy, have you changed. You usta be tall, now you're short. You usta be thin, now you're fat. You usta have hair, now you're bald!"

The other guy says, "My name isn't Joe."

The first guy says, "You changed your name, too?"

Young Wife

Two old friends are sitting around talking. The first guy says, "Henry, I'm a good friend but I gotta ask you how come you married a woman forty years younger than you? You gotta realize she married you for your money."

The second guy says," I know that—but she can drive at night."

Henpecked

At the entrance to the Pearly Gates there are hundreds of guys waiting to get in. Saint Peter says to them, "I want all henpecked husbands to line up on my left and all the non-henpecked husbands to line up on my right."

All the men line up on the left in the henpecked line, except one little old guy who lines up on the right in the non-henpecked line. Saint Peter walks over to him and says, "My good man, are you sure you're in the right line?"

The old man says, "Of course! My wife told me to stand here."

The Bank

A crusty old man walks into a bank and says to a woman at the teller window, "I want to open a damn checking account."

The astonished teller replies, "I beg your pardon, Sir. I must have misunderstood you. What did you say?"

"Listen up, damn it," he said. "I want to open a damn checking account now!"

The teller says, "I'm very sorry, but that kind of language is not tolerated in this bank." The teller leaves the window and goes over to the bank manager to inform him of the situation. The manager agrees that the teller does not have to listen to foul language.

They both return to the window and the manager asks the old guy, "Sir, what seems to be the problem here?"

The man says, "I just won fifty million bucks in the lottery and I want to open a damn checking account in this damn bank."

"I see," says the manager, "and is this bitch giving you a hard time?"

Don't Count Out the Old Guys

Bob, a wealthy seventy-year-old widower, shows up at the country club with a beautiful and very sexy twenty-five-year-old blonde. She hangs over Bob's arm and listens intently to every word.

His buddies at the club are all aghast. They corner him and ask, "Bob, how did you get that trophy girlfriend?"

Bob replies, "Girlfriend? She's my wife."

They continue to ask, "So, how did you persuade her to marry you?"

Bob says, "I lied about my age."

His friends respond, "What do you mean? Did you tell her you were only fifty?"

Bob smiles and says, "No, I told her I was ninety."

Senior Moments

An elderly Floridian calls 911 on her cell phone to report that her car has been broken into. She is hysterical as she explains her situation to the dispatcher: "They've stolen the stereo, the steering wheel, the brake pedal and even the accelerator," she cries.

The dispatcher says, "Stay calm. An officer is on the way."

A few minutes later, the officer radios in. "Disregard," he says, "She got into the back seat by mistake."

A little old lady was running up and down the halls in a nursing home. As she ran, she would flip up the hem of her nightgown and say, "Supersex."

She approached an elderly man in a wheelchair, and flipping her gown at him, she said "Supersex." He sat silently for a moment or two and finally answered, "I'll take the soup."

I Remember It Well

An older couple was lying in bed one night. The husband was falling asleep but the wife was in a romantic mood and wanted to talk. She said, "You used to hold my hand when we were courting."

Wearily, the husband reached across, held her hand for a second and tried to get back to sleep.

A few moments later, she said, "Then, you used to kiss me."

Mildly irritated, he reached across, gave her a peck on her cheek and settled down to sleep.

Thirty seconds later she said, "Then, you used to bite my neck."

Angrily, he threw back the covers and got out of bed.

"Where are you going?" she asked.

"To get my teeth," he replied.

———

Eighty-year-old Bessie bursts into the rec room of the retirement home. She holds her clenched fist in the air and announces, "Anyone who can guess what's in my hand can have sex with me tonight."

An elderly gentleman in the rear shouts out, "An elephant?"

Bessie thinks a minute and says, "Close enough."

———

Sweet Wife

An old guy is invited to his friend's house for dinner. After his wife finishes serving dinner and is in the kitchen cleaning up, his friend says to him, "You know Charlie, I gotta tell you it's amazing that after all these years you still address your wife in those endearing terms.You call her Honey Lamb, Sweetness, Lamb Chop, Pussy Cat. …How come?"

The old guy says, "I forgot her name ten years ago!"

———

The Elderly Ladies

Two elderly ladies had been friends for decades. Over the years, they shared all kinds of activities. Lately, their activities were limited to playing cards. One day, they were playing cards when one lady looked at the other and said, "Now don't get mad at me, I've thought and thought and can't think of your name."

For three minutes, her friend just stared at her. Finally, she said, "How soon do you need to know?"

———

Rotten Food

A dietician was once addressing an audience in Chicago. He said, "The material we put in our stomachs is awful. Soft drinks erode the lining of our stomachs. Chinese food is loaded with MSG. Vegetables can be disastrous, and we don't realize the long- term effects caused by germs in our drinking water. Can anyone tell me what food it is that causes the most grief and suffering for years after eating it?"

A seventy-five-year-old man in the front row stood up and said," A wedding cake?"

The Cruise

An old lady was standing at the railing of a cruise ship, holding her hat on tightly so it wouldn't blow off in the wind. A gentleman approached her and said, "Pardon me, I don't intend to be forward, but did you know that your dress is blowing up in this high wind?"

"Yes, I know," said the lady. "I need both hands to hold onto this hat."

"But, Madame, you must know that your privates are exposed!" said the man.

The woman looked down, then back up at the man and replied, "Sir, anything you see down there is eighty-five years old. I just bought this hat yesterday."

Anyone Can Get a Driver's License

Two elderly ladies were out driving in a large car. They could hardly see over the dashboard. As they were cruising along, they came to an intersection. The stoplight was red, but they just went on through.

The woman in the passenger seat thought to herself, "I must be losing it. I could have sworn we just went through a red light."

After a few more minutes, they came to another intersection, the light was red again, and the old lady driver went right through it. At the next intersection, sure enough, the light was red and they went right through it.

Finally, the passenger turned to the other woman and said, "Mildred, did you know that we just ran through three red lights in a row? You could have killed us both!"

Mildred turned to her and said, "Oh, crap, am I driving?"

Not of this World

As a senior citizen was driving down the freeway, her car phone rang. Answering, she heard her husband's voice urging her, "Helen, I just heard on the news that there is a car going the wrong way on Interstate 77. Please be careful!"

"Hell," said Helen, "It's not one car. It's hundreds of them!"

The Bathroom

An eighty-year-old man went for his annual checkup and the doctor said, “Friend, for your age you’re the best I’ve seen.”

The old fella replied, “Yep, it comes from clean living. I live a very clean, spiritual life.”

The doctor asked, “What makes you say that?”

The old man replied, “Well, if I didn’t lead a clean life, the Lord wouldn’t turn on the bathroom light for me every time I get up in the middle of the night.”

The doc was concerned and asked, “You mean when you get up during the night to go to the bathroom, the Lord turns the light on for you?”

“Yep,” said the old man.

The doctor didn’t say anything else, but when the old man’s wife came in for her checkup, he said, “I just want you to know that your husband is in fine physical shape but I’m worried about his mental condition. He told me that every night when he gets up to go to the bathroom, the Lord turns the light on for him.”

“He what?” she cried.

The doctor repeated what he told her about the Lord turning on the light for him every time he goes to the bathroom at night.

“Aha!” she exclaimed. “So he’s the one who’s been peeing in the refrigerator!”

Never Felt Better

An eighty-year-old man is having his annual checkup. The doctor asks him how he’s feeling. “I’ve never been better!" he replied. "I've got an eighteen-year-old bride who's pregnant and having my child! What do you think about that?"

The doctor considers this for a moment, then says, "Well, let me tell you a story. I know a guy who is an avid hunter. One day, he's in a hurry and accidentally grabs his umbrella instead of his gun. So he's in the woods and suddenly a grizzly bear appears in front of him! He raises his umbrella, points it at the bear, and squeezes the handle. The bear drops dead in front of him."

The old man says, "That's impossible! Someone else must have shot the bear."

"Exactly."

Viagra Stories

An elderly gentlemen went to a local drug store and asked the pharmacist for Viagra. The pharmacist asked, "How many?"

The man replied, "Just a few, maybe a half dozen. I cut each one into four pieces."

The pharmacist said, "That's too small a dose. That won't be enough to get you through sex."

The old fellow said, "Oh, I'm so old, I don't think about sex anymore. I just want it to stick out far enough so I don't pee on my shoes!"

A truck carrying a shipment of Viagra was hijacked in New York City. The police have put out an alert—if you spot the truck, notify authorities at once. Do not approach! These are hardened criminals!

———

Q.What's the difference between Niagara and Viagra?
A. Niagara falls.

———

Of course you heard of the Viagra computer virus: it turns your three-inch floppy into a hard disk.

———

This guy spent too much money on Viagra. Now, he's hard up.

———

Did you hear about the first death caused by Viagra? A guy took 12 pills and his wife died.

———

Men taking iron supplements with Viagra may cause them to spin around and point.

———

Unconfirmed reports tells us that a man who overdosed on Viagra died, but they couldn't close the coffin lid for three days.

———

Bread with Viagra as an added ingredient is being marketed by a New England bakery under the name of "Pepperidge Firm!"

There are plans to raise the Titanic. Experts plan to pump it full of Viagra and expect it to rise from the ocean bottom by itself.

The funeral parlors are happy about the deaths caused by the overdose of Viagra. Lots of stiffs means an upswing in business.

A man picking up his prescription for Viagra complained at the cost of ten dollars for each pill. His wife was with him at the time, and exclaimed, "Forty dollars a year isn't that expensive!"

The Poker Game

Five friends play a poker game once a week for many years. One of the guys suffers a heart attack and passes away while playing a game. The other four guys are very upset by his passing and say to his wife, "We know you want Irving cremated, but we could still include him in our weekly card games. We could put his ashes in an urn and put the urn on the card table whenever we play. That way, it would seem like Irving is still with us."

The wife agrees and she suggests the group meet once a month at her house for their game. When they arrive to play, the urn is set on the table. As the game gets more intense and the stakes get higher, the guys smoke and flick their ashes into the urn. This goes on for months as they keep playing and flicking their ashes in the urn.

One day after the game when Irving's wife is cleaning up, she picks up the urn to put it back on the mantle of the fireplace. She looks into the urn and says, "You know, it's hard to believe, but I think Irving is putting on weight!"

The Krupnick Diamond

A passenger on a plane sits down next to a very large woman who has an extremely large diamond on her finger. The man says, "Pardon me, but I have never seen a ring with such a huge diamond!"

The woman nods and says, "Yes, this is the Krupnick Diamond. It has a long history and it also comes with a curse."

Fascinated, the man says, "If you don't mind me asking, what is the curse?"

The woman says, "Mr. Krupnick!"

What Insurance Do You Have?

Ethel and Mabel, two elderly widows, were watching the folks go by from their park bench.

Ethel said, "You know, Mabel, I've been reading a sex and marriage book and they talk about something called 'mutual orgasm'! Tell me, Mabel, when your husband was alive, did you two ever have mutual orgasm?"

Mabel thought for a long while. Finally, she shook her head and said, "No, I think we had State Farm."

How Sweet It Was

Three old ladies were sitting side by side at their retirement home reminiscing. The first lady recalled shopping at the greengrocer's and demonstrated with her hands the length and thickness of a cucumber she could buy for a penny.

The second lady said, "Onions used to be much bigger and cheaper, too," and she demonstrated the size of two big onions she could buy for a penny a piece.

The third old lady said, "I can't hear a word you're saying, but I remember the guy you're talking about."

I Need a Ride

Two elderly ladies were sitting on the front porch. One lady turned and asked, "Do you still get horny?"

The other replies, "Oh, sure I do."

The first lady asks, "What do you do about it?"

The second old lady replies, "I suck a lifesaver."

After a few moments, the first old lady asks, "Who drives you to the beach?"

The Little Old Lady

There was a preacher whose wife was expecting a baby.

The preacher went to the congregation and asked for a raise. After much consideration and discussion, they passed a rule that whenever the preacher's family expanded, so would his paycheck.

After six children, this started to get expensive and the congregation decided to hold another meeting to discuss the preacher's salary. There was much yelling and bickering about how much the clergyman's additional children were costing the church.

Finally, the preacher got up and spoke to the crowd. "Having children is an act of God!" Silence fell upon the congregation. No one dared to challenge that thought.

Then in the back of the room, a little old lady stood up, and in her frail voice said, "Snow and rain are also acts of God, but when we get too much, we wear rubbers!"

Still Looking

A lonely woman, aged seventy, decided it was time to get married. She put an ad in the paper that read:

HUSBAND WANTED! MUST BE IN MY AGE GROUP (70's), MUST NOT BEAT ME, MUST NOT RUN AROUND ON ME AND MUST STILL BE GOOD IN BED!

ALL APPLICANTS PLEASE APPLY IN PERSON.

On the second day she heard the doorbell. Much to her dismay, she opened the door to see a gray-haired gentleman sitting in a wheelchair. He had no arms or legs.

The old woman said, "You're not really asking me to consider you, are you? Just look at you. ...You have no legs!"

The old man smiled, "Therefore I cannot run around on you!"

She snorted. "You don't have any hands, either!"

Again the old man smiled, "Nor can I beat you!"

She raised an eyebrow and gazed intently. "Are you still good in bed?"

With that, the old gentleman leaned back, beamed a big broad smile and said, "I rang the doorbell, didn't I?"

Being Retired

Working people frequently ask retired people what they do to make their days interesting. I went to the store the other day. I was only in there for about five minutes but when I came out therewas a city cop writing out a parking ticket.

I went up to him and said, "Come on, buddy, how about giving a senior a break?"

He ignored me and continued writing the ticket. I called him a Nazi.

He glared at me and started writing another ticket for having worn tires.

So I called him a piece of horse shit. He finished the second ticket and put it on the windshield with the first. Then he started writing a third ticket.

This went on for about 20 minutes.. the more I abused him, the more tickets he wrote. I didn't give a crap. My car was parked around the corner.

I try to have a little fun each day now that I'm retired. It's important at my age.

Who Are You?

This old man is walking down the street and sees a guy coming toward him who he seems to recognize. He says, "Hi, Irving!"

The other guy says, "I'm not Irving."

The man says, "You look just like Irving Goldberg who I spent last winter with at the baths in Hot Springs!"

The other guy says, "I was never in Hot Springs!"

The man says, "I know, you're Philly Greenwald from the Roni Plaza in Miami!"

The other guy says, "I was never at the Roni Plaza!"

The man says, "Aren't you Fred Schwartz? Didn't we play poker every night for two weeks at the Concord Hotel?"

The other guy says, "No, I haven't been to the Concord Hotel in years!"

The man says, "Then who are you?"

The other guy says, "Schmuck, I'm your brother, Jack!!"

The Dress

Irving comes home from work early. He goes up to the bedroom and is surprised to see his wife in bed, stark naked. He said, "Vot's going on? How come you're not dressed and out shopping?"

She says, "Vell, I don't have any nice clothes to wear!"

He says, "Vot are you talking about?" He goes over to her closet, opens the door and says, "Vot do you mean you don't have clothes? Look!! You got a pink dress, a blue dress, a yellow dress, hello Sidney, a gray dress…"

Still Driving

A man was telling his friend, "I've sure gotten old! I've had two bypass surgeries, a hip replacement, new knees, diabetes and fought prostate cancer. I'm half blind, can't hear very well, take forty medications that make me dizzy and subject to blackouts. I also have bouts with dementia, have poor circulation, can hardly feel my hands and feet anymore and have lost all my friends. But thank God, I still have my Florida driver's license!"

The 104-Year-Old Lady

Reporters were interviewing a 104-year-old woman. One of the reporters asked, "What do you think is the best thing about being 104?"

The woman thought for a moment and then replied, "No peer pressure."

CHAPTER 6

GOLF STORIES

"Golf is a game whose aim is to hit a very small ball into a smaller hole, with weapons singularly designed for the purpose."

Winston Churchill

For Golfers Only

I love to play golf. I love golf almost as much as I love comedy. They say that golf has replaced sex. Of course, only men over sixty are saying it. Golf is a great game. You spend your life with hookers and your wife doesn't say a word.

The trouble with golf is that by the time you can afford to lose a few balls, you can't hit them that far anymore! I found out that the secret of missing a tree is to aim straight at it!

My wife complains to me and says, "On the golf course, you can walk thirty-six holes and at home, you won't even get up for a glass of water!" She feels that golf is great exercise. Especially getting in and out of the golf cart!

I was playing golf just the other day with a few friends. The first player teed off and hit the ball into a clump of trees. On the fairway, he swung again and sliced a new ball into a deep water hazard. A third swing resulted in a new ball flying over a fence onto a busy street. I told him he should use old balls. He replied, "I never had any old balls!"

Favorite Golf Stories

I bought a dozen golf balls at a store the other day. The sales clerk said, "Shall I wrap them up?" I told him, "No, I'll drive them home!"

I play golf with a Scottish friend named Dennis. He gave up golf after twenty years. He lost his ball! I meet a lot of guys on the golf course. One of my friends needs psychological help—he actually treats golf like a game!

I know I'm getting better at golf because I'm hitting fewer spectators.

President Gerald R. Ford

When I go out to play golf, I always consider my wife and ask if she has any plans. I ask, "Golf course or intercourse?"

Her answer is always the same. She says, "Don't forget to wear a warm sweater."

I was in the men's locker room getting dressed. One of my friends looked at me in surprise and asked, "How come you're wearing panty hose?"

I answered, "Ever since my wife found them in the glove compartment of my car."

I asked my caddy if he thought it was a sin to play on religious holidays. He said, "Any day *you* play is a sin!"

(Ouch!)

It Really Hurts

Four guys are getting ready to tee off. On an adjacent tee, four women are also teeing off. The first woman hits a shank and hits this guy very low. He drops to the ground, clutching himself and in obvious pain.

The woman rushes over yelling, "I'm so sorry, it's the first time I'm playing. Let me help you, I'm a physical therapist."

The guy is still rolling around in pain, saying, "Just leave me alone." Then she jumps on him, opens his fly and shoves her hand into his pants. She's rubbing, squeezing, and massaging.

Then she says, "Doesn't that feel better?"

He says, "It feels great, but you hit me in the finger!"

Golf Fantasy

This grandfather is playing golf with his eight-year-old grandson. The little boy hits his tee shot into a nearby lake. They start walking down to the lake to see if they can retrieve the ball. As they pass a big rock near the lake, they hear a voice saying, "HELLOOO."

They both stop, look around and to their surprise, they see a frog sitting on a rock. The frog says, "Don't be afraid, I'm really a princess that was cursed by a wicked witch.

Sir, if you would just kiss me on my amphibious lips, I will turn into a beautiful princess and do your bidding for the rest of your life."

The grandfather walks over to the rock, picks up the frog and puts it into his pocket.

His grandson is amazed. He says, "Grandpa, all you have to do is kiss the frog on her lips and she will turn into a beautiful princess and do what ever you want her to do, for the rest of your life."

The grandfather says to him, "At my age, I'd rather have a talking frog!"

Golf Heaven

Two old guys that have been friends for over 50 years are talking about golf. One says, "You know, Harry, I wonder if there are golf courses in Heaven."

Morris says, "I really don't know, but the first one of us that gets there should try to contact the other."

A week later Harry passes on. Three weeks after that, Morris is sitting home, dejected at having lost his best friend, when all of a sudden he hears a voice.

"Morris! Morris, it's me, Harry, speaking to you from Heaven."

"Is it really you, Harry?" Morris asks.

"Yes, it is, and I have good news and bad news for you. First the good news. Golf is fantastic up here. They have the most magnificent courses! The bad news Is that you have a starting time tomorrow at 9 a.m!"

A Winner

A very attractive woman has been playing with this group of men for a few years and has never won. This particular day they reach the 18th hole and all she needs to do is sink her putt to win. The putt is about 15 feet from the hole, so she really wants to win the match.

She says to the guys, "Whoever can line up my ball so it goes into the cup, I'll sleep with tonight."

The guys are all excited because she is really beautiful. The first guy gets behind the ball and says it's going to break right. She putts and misses.

The second guy says its going to break left at the hole. She putts and misses.

The last guy gets down behind the ball, takes a couple of seconds, then says. "Ah, it's a gimmee!!"

The Five Iron

This guy walks into his doctor's office with a five iron wrapped around his neck and in great pain. The doctor asks him what happened.

He answers, "I'm playing with my wife and she hits a ball out of bounds into this field and insists on finding the ball. So, we start looking for it. We can't find it. Then I happen to see a cow about 25 feet from me swishing his tail. On closer observation, I see a white object that looks like a ball in the ass of the cow. So, I walk over gently, pick up the cow's tail and sure enough, I see a ball. All I said to my wife was, "This looks like yours!"

Questions

This couple is having breakfast and the wife says, "Honey, can I ask you a hypothetical question? If I died, would you remarry?"

The husband answers, "Well, I really love you and I enjoy marriage, so probably yes."

The wife asks, "Would she move into our house?"

The husband says, "Yeah, I would let her move in."

The wife continues her questions and asks, "Would you let her sleep in our bed?"

The husband says, "I guess so."

The wife asks again, "Would you let her use my golf clubs?"

The husband answers, "Absolutely not."

The wife says, "Wait a minute. You'd let her move into the house and sleep in our bed, but you wouldn't let her use my clubs? Why not?"

The husband answers, "Because she's left handed!"

Marooned

This guy is marooned on a desert island for years. He's on the beach looking out to sea when he jumps up and can't believe his eyes. Coming out of the surf is a beautiful woman wearing a wet suit with an unbelievable body.

He runs down to the shore to greet her. She's stunned to see a man standing in front of her in tattered clothes, a long beard and completely bedraggled. Excitedly, he says, "Thank God, finally another human being."

She says, "How long have you been stranded here?"

He says, “For years, I don’t even know how long. Where did you come from?”

She answers, “Our launch is around the next cove.”

Then, feeling sorry for him she says, “Would you like a cigarette?”

He says, “Yes,” so she pulls the zipper down on the arm of her wet suit, takes out a cigarette, lights it and hands it to him. He can’t believe it.

Then she says, “Would you like a beer?” She pulls the zipper down on her left leg of her wet suit and pulls out a beer. The guy is totally amazed.

She says, “I can’t believe you’ve been here for so many years. Would you like to play around?”

He says, “Oh, my God! Don’t tell me you have a set of golf clubs in there, too!”

Tiger and Stevie

Tiger Woods walks into this lounge and Stevie Wonder, his favorite entertainer, is sitting by the bar. So Tiger goes over and starts talking. He says, “Hi, Stevie, I’m Tiger Woods.”

Stevie is really happy and says, “Hey, my man, how you doin? Still winning all those tournaments?”

Tiger replies, “I’m doing well. How about you?”

Stevie says, “You know, I’m an avid golfer.”

Tiger says, “Really?”

Stevie says, “Yeah, I’m a six handicap.”

Tiger is amazed and says, “Stevie, are you putting me on?”

Stevie answers, “No, in fact, I’ll bet you $10,000 that I can beat you.”

Tiger says, "C'mon, Stevie, you know I will beat you." Finally, he says, "Okay, I'll play you if you want to be such a wiseguy. When do you want to play?"

Stevie says, "Pick any night!"

No Surprises

A bachelor tried to take a vacation every summer. He was a golf nut and spent two weeks at Hilton Head. Last summer, he met a woman out there and fell head over heels in love with her.

On the last night of his vacation, the two of them went out to dinner and had a serious talk about how they would continue the relationship. They agreed that total honesty was important so there would be no surprises later that could destroy their love.

"It's only fair to warn you that I'm a total golf nut," Ed said to his lady friend. "I eat, sleep, and breathe golf, so if that's a problem, you'd better say so now."

"Well, if we are being honest with each other, here goes," she replied. "I'm a hooker."

Ed thinks for a moment and then says, "I see. You know I can't help you with that. It's probably because you're not keeping your wrists straight when you tee off."

On Time

Four guys who worked together always golfed as a group at 6:30 a.m. every Sunday. Unfortunately, one of them got transferred out of town and they talked about getting another guy to play.

A woman standing near the tee said, "Hey, I like to golf, can I join the group?"

They were hesitant, but they said she could play once with them and they'd see how it worked out. They told her to be there at 6:30 a.m.

She showed up on time and wound up setting a course record with a seven under par round. The guys were happy and congratulated her. They invited her back the next week and she showed up again at 6:30 a.m. This time, she played left-handed and matched her seven under par score of the previous week.

They had a beer after the round and one of the guys asked her, "How do you decide whether to play right-handed or left-handed?"

She said, "That's easy. Before I leave for the golf course, I pull the covers off my husband, who sleeps in the nude. If his member points to the right, I golf right-handed; if it points to the left, I golf left-handed."

One of the guys asked, "What if it's pointed straight up?"

She said, "Then I'll be here at 6:45."

The Steam Room

I was invited by a friend of mine to play golf at his golf course. Since we got there early, we decided to take a steam bath before playing. We went to the men's locker room, got undressed, threw a towel around us and off we went to the steam room.

We didn't notice that the steam room was filled with women. The women saw us and started to scream! My friend said, "Omigod, I forgot that today is Ladies' Day!"

We were standing there like two jerks and one woman said, "That's not my husband!"

Another woman said, "That's not my husband, either!"

Finally, one woman said, "They aren't even members of the club!"

A Golfer's Variety

A man came home from work and was greeted by his wife, dressed in a sexy little nightie.

"Tie me up," she purred, "and you can do anything you want."

So he tied her up and went out for a round of golf.

A golfer asked his friend, "Why are you so late?"

The friend replied, "It's Sunday. I had to toss a coin between going to church or playing golf. It took twenty-five tosses to get it right!"

The Secret

A gushy reporter told Jack Nicklaus, "You are spectacular, and your name is synonymous with the game of golf. You really know your way around the course. What's your secret?"

Nicklaus replied, "The holes are numbered."

Concentration

A young man and a priest are playing together. At a short par-three the priest asks, "What are you going to use on this hole, my son?"

The young man says, "An eight-iron, Father. How about you?"

The priest says, "I'm going to hit a soft seven and pray."

The young man hits his eight-iron and puts the ball on the green. The priest tops his seven-iron and dribbles the ball out a few yards.

The young man says, "I don't know about you, Father, but in my church when we pray, we keep our heads down."

Great Shot!

Police were called to an apartment and found a man holding a bloody three-iron, standing over a lifeless woman.

The detective asked, "Sir, is that your wife?"

"Yes," the man responded.

"Did you hit her with that golf club?"

"Yes, yes, I did." The man began to sob, dropped the club, and put his hands on his face.

"How many times did you hit her?"

"I don't remember."

The detective said, "I can't complete my report unless you tell me."

"I don't know...five, six, maybe seven times. Just put me down for a five."

A Golf Story

An older Sun City couple made a deal that whoever died first would come back and inform the other of the afterlife. Their biggest fear was that there was no afterlife.

After a long life, the husband was the first to go, and true to his word, he made contact. "Mary...Mary... ."

"Is that you, Fred?" she asked.

Fred said, "Yes, I've come back like we agreed."

"What's it like?"

"Well, I get up in the morning, I have sex. I have breakfast, off to the golf course, I have sex. I bathe in the sun, then I have sex twice. I have lunch, another romp around the golf course, then sex pretty much all afternoon. After supper, golf course again. Then have sex until late at night. The next day it starts again."

Mary says, "Oh, Fred, you surely must be in heaven."

"Not exactly, I'm a rabbit on a golf course in Des Moines."

Golf and Marriage

An eighty-five-year-old couple, married for sixty years, die in a car crash. They had been in good health mainly due to the wife's interest in health food. When they reach the pearly gates, St. Peter takes them to their mansion.

The old man asks, "How much will this cost?"

St. Peter replies, "It's free. Remember this is heaven."

Next, they go out back to see the golf course. They would have golfing privileges every day. The old man asks, "What are the greens fees?"

St. Peter says, "It's free!" Next, they go to the clubhouse and see the lavish buffet lunch.

The old man asks, "How much is it to eat?"

St. Peter says, "Don't you understand? This is Heaven. It's free!"

The old man asks, "Well, where are the low fat and low cholesterol foods?"

St. Peter replies, "You can eat as much as you like of whatever you want and you never get fat or sick. This is Heaven!"

The old man looks at his wife and says, "You and your fucking bran muffins. I could have been here ten years ago!"

Golf is a Rough Game

A businessman was attending a conference in Africa. He had a free day and wanted to play a round of golf. There was a golf course nearby.

After a short ride, he arrived and asked the pro when he could go out.

The pro said, "Sure. ...What's your handicap?"

Not wanting to admit he had an eighteen handicap, he decided to cut it to sixteen. The pro called a caddy and told him his handicap was sixteen. The caddy picked up the man's bag and a large rifle.

They got to the first hole, a par four. The caddy said, "Please avoid the trees to the left."

The man hooked his first shot right into the trees. He found the ball and was about to swing when he heard the loud crack of a rifle. A large snake fell dead from the tree above his head.

The caddy stood next to him with his gun still smoking and said, "That's the mamba, the most poisonous snake in Africa."

They moved on to the second hole. The caddy said, "Avoid the large rocks on your left."

Of course, the man's ball went slicing into the rocks. As he went to pick up his ball, he heard the loud crack of the caddy's rifle again. A huge lion fell at his feet.

The caddy said, "I've saved your life again!"

The third hole was a par three with a lake in front of the green. The businessman had a shot, but he had to place one foot in the water to be able to hit the ball.

Just as he was about to hit the ball, a large crocodile emerged from the water and bit his foot off. As he fell to the ground in pain, he glanced up and saw the caddy standing there with the rifle looking very unconcerned.

"Why didn't you shoot?" asked the man.

"I'm sorry," answered the caddy, "but this is the 17th hole and you don't get a shot here!"

Chapter 7

MARRIAGE

"Marriage is a great institution. But who wants to live in an institution?"

Half the jokes in the history of the world have been about married people. I always use the line, "I've been in love with the same woman for twenty-eight years. If my wife ever finds out, she'll kill me."

I married her for her looks, but not the ones she's been giving me lately!

It's a fact that single people die younger. Marriage is healthier. If you're looking for a long life and a slow death, get married!

My wife and I never go to bed mad. We stay up and talk until the problem is resolved. Last year we didn't get to sleep until May.

We're getting older now and we decided last year that we had to start thinking about burial plots. They are very expensive, but for her birthday, I bought my wife a plot. This year she complained that I didn't buy her anything for her birthday. I told her she didn't even use the present I got her last year.

My friend told me if his wife really loved him, she would have married someone else! My friend asked me if it was true that married men live longer than single men. I told him, "No, it only seems longer!"

My wife said to me, "Let's not stay home all the time. Let's go out three times a week."

I told her, "Good idea. You go out Monday, Wednesday, and Friday and I'll go out Tuesday, Thursday and Saturday!

My wife keeps telling me that she gave me the best years of her life. If those were the best, I really worry about the years coming up!

The Marriage Game

I've been married for thirty happy years and thirty out of fifty ain't bad.

Milton Berle

You know what it means to come home at night to a beautiful woman standing in the doorway, holding a glass of wine for you? You go into the house, the table is set with beautiful candelabras, the music is soft and inviting. You know what it means?

It means you're in the wrong house!

I said to my wife, "Fun and sex have gone out of our marriage."

She said, "Lets discuss it during the next commercial."

A Monologue

I'm married a long time and I still don't understand women. A woman can pour boiling wax on her thighs. When it drys, she rips it off, pulling the skin with the hair off by the roots. But she can still be afraid of a little spider.

I'd like to be a woman for one day. I wanna know how it feels to retain water, to get pissed off for no apparent reason, to change my mind every minute of the day, and to tell all my innermost secrets to my gay hairdresser.

I WANNA DO THINGS THAT WOMEN DO. I wanna go to the bathroom in groups. Can you imagine men doing that?

(With feeling) "Hey, Louie, Tony, Mikey. I gotta go to the toilet, join me!"

Anniversary Breakfast

My wife said to me on our 30th anniversary, "Why don't we go back to the hotel where we had our honeymoon?"

I said, "That would be great!" So we did.

The next morning I said to my wife, "Since we're reliving the past, why don't we do the same thing that we did for breakfast years ago?"

My wife said, "You mean, eat breakfast naked?" So I ordered room service.

When the food came and the bellhop left, we both took off our pajamas and sat down naked for an exciting meal. As we were eating, my wife looked at me and said, "You know honey, I still get excited when I look at you. In fact, right now my breasts feel hot and tingly."

I looked at her and said, "There's a reason for that. Your left breast is in the coffee and your right one is in the oatmeal."

Grandma

This granddaughter goes to visit her Grandma. Grandpa just died and Grandma is very sad. Her granddaughter tries to console her. She says, "After all, Grandpa was 87 years old and you had a wonderful life together."

Grandma says, "I know, but he was in such great shape we had sex every Sunday."

The granddaughter is stunned and says, "You had sex every Sunday? What happened to him?"

Grandma says, "He had a heart attack. We were making love on Sunday. We used to start at 8:45 a.m. and we did it to the rhythm of the church bells down the street. It was so nice, in with a ding and out with a dong!"

The granddaughter says, "So what happened?"

Grandma says, "Whoever thought the ice cream truck would come by at 9 a.m.?"

A Matter of Values

A man returning home a day early from a business trip got into a taxi at the airport. It was after midnight.

While on route to his home, he asked the cabbie if he would be a witness. The man suspected his wife was having an affair and he intended to catch her in the act. For $100, the cabbie agreed.

Quietly arriving at the house, the husband and cabbie tiptoed into the bedroom. The husband switched on the lights, yanked the blanket back and there was his wife in bed with another man.

The husband put a gun to the naked man's head. The wife shouted, "Don't do it! This man has been very generous. ...I lied when I told you I inherited money. He paid for the Corvette I bought for you. He paid for our new cabin cruiser. He paid for our house at the lake. He paid for our country club membership, and he even pays the monthly dues."

Shaking his head from side to side, the husband slowly lowered the gun. He looked over at the cab driver and said, "What would you do?"

The cabbie said, "I'd cover his ass up with that blanket before he catches a cold."

Money In The Bank

A young bride approached her waiting husband on their wedding night and demanded $30 for their first love-making encounter. In his highly aroused state, he agreed. This scenario was repeated each time they made love for the next thirty years, him thinking it was a cute way for her to buy things she wanted.

Arriving home around noon one day, she found her husband in a very drunken state. Over the next few minutes she heard the ravages of financial ruin caused by corporate downsizing and its effects on her fifty-year-old executive husband.

Calmly, she handed him a bank book showing deposits and interest nearly totaling $1 million, and informing him he was the largest stockholder in the bank. She told him for thirty years she had charged him each time they had sex and this was the result of her investments.

By now, he was distraught and beat his head on the side of the car. She asked him why he was so disappointed at such good news.

He replied, "If I had known what you were doing, I would have given you all of my business!"

Horse Sense

This guy is sitting on his couch, watching a football game on TV. His wife comes up behind him, rolls up a newspaper and raps him as hard as she can on the side of his head.

He leaps up, grabbing his ear, and yells out, "What the hell did you do that for?"

His wife very angrily replies, “You want to know why? I’ll tell you why! This morning, I took your pants to the cleaners to be pressed. I don’t usually go through your pockets but I wanted to make sure that you didn’t leave any stuff in the pockets. I found a slip of paper that said ‘Mary Jane’ on it.”

Her husband says, “That’s why you hit me? Well, that note was a reminder for me. That’s the name of a horse that’s running at Belmont Race track on Saturday. Mary Jane is the name of the horse I’m betting on.”

The wife says, “Oh, I’m so sorry. I never should have mistrusted you.”

A few nights later, her husband is watching another game on TV. This time she walks behind him and hits him on the side of his head with a frying pan. He goes flying off the couch. Blood is flowing from his ear. He is totally stunned.

Finally, after a few minutes, he regains consciousness and yells at her, “What did you hit me for?”

She says, “Your horse just called!”

Work Around the House

My wife was really nudging me one day. She said, “Honey, you promised to fix the leaky faucet.”

I said to her, “Do you see ‘plumber’ inscribed on my forehead?”

She said, “What about the broken stair?”

I said, “Do you see ‘carpenter’ written on my forehead?”

She said, “What about painting the library? You promised you would do it.”

I said, "Do I look like I have 'painter' burned into my forehead?"

Finally, I got so mad from all the nudging that I ran out to the local bar. After three drinks, I realized that I'd been a little bit nasty, so I went back home. My wife was sitting in the living room with a big smile on her face.

I said to her, "Listen, I was wrong, I'll do all the repairs."

She said, "Don't bother, as soon as you left, a young man came by and saw me crying. I told him what had happened and he said he would be happy to fix everything. When he finished, I said to him, "Would you like me to bake you a cake or would you like to go to bed with me?"

I said, "So what happened?"

She said, "Do I look like I have Betty Crocker written on my forehead?"

Macho Man

A typical macho man married a typical good-looking lady and after the wedding, he laid down the following rules:

"I'll be home when I want, if I want and at what time I want, and I don't expect any hassle from you. I expect a great dinner to be on the table unless I tell you that I won't be home for dinner. I'll go hunting, fishing, boozing and card-playing when I want with my old buddies and don't you give me a hard time about it. Those are my rules. Any comments?"

His new bride said, "No, that's fine with me. Just understand that there will be sex here at seven o'clock every night—whether you're here or not."

Making Amends

A husband and his wife are having a fight at the breakfast table. The husband gets up in a rage and says, "And you're no good in bed, either," and storms out of the house.

After some time, he realizes he was nasty and decides to make amends and rings her up. She comes to the phone after many rings, and the irritated husband says, "What took you so long to answer the phone?"

She says, "I was in bed."

"In bed this early, doing what?"

"Getting a second opinion!"

The Trap

Saul and Sarah Firnbaum were on a cruise. For forty years, they had saved up to go on this cruise. They were having a wonderful time when the ship was was hit by a violent rainstorm! They decided to go back to their cabin, which was on the upper deck of the ship. As they made their way back to the cabin, a huge wave smashed into the ship, carrying Sarah over the side and into the water.

Saul ran to the rail, barely being able to stand due to the storm. He was yelling at the top of his lungs for someone to help, but to no avail. After the storm subsided, the ship came to a standstill while the crew searched for Sarah. After many hours they gave up the search.

Saul was completely devastated. On return of the ship to home port, Saul disembarked and went home and into seclusion. He would talk to no one. Finally, after few months, he started to resume his life.

One morning, he received a telephone call from the Coast Guard. The voice on the phone said, "Sir, this is Captain Jon Smythe from the United States Coast Guard. We have good news and bad news to give to you."

Saul, with some trepidation in his voice said, "What's the bad news?"

The captain said, "Well, sir, we have located the body of your wife."

Saul said, "I see, and what could be the good news?"

"Well, sir, after an examination of the body, which is a Coast Guard priority, we found a huge perfect pearl in your wife's vagina. We want to know what you would like us to do."

There was silence on the phone for a few minutes. Then Saul said, "Send me the pearl, reset the trap, and throw her back in the ocean!"

Controlling Bitch

This guy is married for many years to one of the most domineering and controlling women. She wants to direct everything he says or does. She is also very hard of hearing.

They are on a road trip to Spokane, Washington. The husband is driving and decides to pull into a gas station to fill up. The attendant comes over to the car and says, "How can I help you?"

The wife says, "What did he say?"

The husband replies, "He said, he wants to help us."

The attendant starts filling up the car with gas and says, "Where are you heading?"

The husband says, "Spokane."

The wife says, "What did he say?"

The husband says, "He wants to know where we're heading."

The attendant then says, "I used to live in Spokane. I had a woman up there who was the worst sex partner I ever had. I mean the worst lay ever!"

The wife again yells out, "What did he say?"

The husband replies, "He says he thinks he knows you!"

The Statue

A woman is in bed with her lover when she hears her husband opening the front door. "Hurry!" she says, "stand in the corner." She quickly rubs baby oil all over him and then she dusts him with talcum powder. "Don't move until I tell you to, just pretend you're a statue."

The husband walks in the room and says, "What's this, honey?"

She replies, "Oh, it's just a statue that I bought. The Smiths bought one for their bedroom. I liked it so much, I got one for us, too."

Later on, they go to bed. Around two in the morning, the husband gets out of bed, goes to the kitchen, and returns with a sandwich and a glass of milk.

"Here," he says to the statue, "Eat something. I stood like an idiot at the Smiths for three days and nobody offered me as much as a glass of water."

Newlyweds

A newlywed couple had only been married for two weeks. The husband, although very much in love, couldn't wait to go out on the town and party with his old buddies. So, he said to his new wife, "Honey, I'll be right back."

"Where are you going, coochy coo?" asked the wife.

"I'm going to the bar, pretty face. I'm going to have a beer."

The wife said, "You want a beer, my love?" She opened the door to the refrigerator and showed him twenty-five different kinds of beer, brands from twelve different countries, including Germany, Holland, Japan, India, and others.

The husband didn't know what to do, and the only thing that he could think of saying was, "Yes, lollipop, but at the bar, you know...they have frozen glasses. ..."

He didn't get to finish the sentence because his wife interrupted him by saying, "You want a frozen glass, puppy face?" She took a huge beer mug out of the freezer, so frozen that she was getting chills just holding it.

The husband, looking a bit pale, said, "Yes, Tootsie Roll, but at the bar they have these hors d'oeuvres that are really delicious. ...I won't be long, I'll be right back. I promise. OK?"

"You want hors d'oeuvres, poochi poo?" She opened the oven and took out five dishes of different hors d'oeuvres: chicken wings, pigs in blankets, mushroom caps, pork strips, and Sweedish meatballs.

"But my sweet honey...at the bar...you know...there's swearing, dirty words and all that..."

"You want dirty words, cutie pie? LISTEN UP, DICK-HEAD! DRINK YOUR FUCKING BEER IN YOUR GODDAMN FROZEN MUG AND EAT YOUR MOTH-ERFUCKING SNACKS, BECAUSE YOU'RE MAR-RIED NOW, AND YOU AREN'T GOING ANYWHERE! GOT IT, ASSHOLE?"

...And they lived happily ever after.

More Monologue

I got married so young, we didn't go on a honeymoon. ...I sent her to camp for the summer.

The reason our marriage has lasted so long is that every morning when we get up, I look her right in the eyes and apologize. I say, "I'm sorry, dear!" It covers me for the whole day.

My wife has always supported me. When I lost my first job, she was there for me. When I went into business and didn't know what I was doing, I went bankrupt and she was there for me. When our first house burnt down, she was there for me.

You know something? She's a f—— ing jinx.

We have four sons. Two lawyers and two defendants.

One son is named Otto. He's dyslexic. This way he only has to remember two letters.

He came to me a few weeks ago and said, "Dad! I gotta get rid of my car."

I said, "Why?"

He said, "It has over 140,000 miles on it."

I said, "Take it to an odometer place, give them a few bucks and they'll turn back the mileage."

I just saw him a couple of days ago and asked him if he sold the car. He said, "Why should I sell it? It only has 6,000 miles on it."

Dave Barry

More Monologues, One-liners and Jokes

We are happily married. We wake up in the middle of the night and laugh at each other.

For our last honeymoon, she said to me, "I'd like to go somewhere that I haven't been in a long time."

I said, "How about the kitchen?"

She treats me like a God. Every meal is a burnt offering!

Henny Youngman

What's in a Name?

We were married a long time. I wanted to get her something really nice, so I went to the Nordstrom's cosmetic department. I said to the saleswoman, "How about some perfume?"

She suggested a very expensive perfume at $150 an ounce. It's called, *Perhaps*.

I said, "For $150 an ounce, it's gotta be for sure!"

I finally got her one of those little love birds, you know yellow, pink, green and really beautiful. She fed it baked beans. Now we have a thunderbird!

She's a big shopper. She speaks fluent Latin: "Veni, Vidi, Visa."

"I came, I saw, I bought."

Her credit card was stolen about six weeks ago. I never reported it.

Whoever stole it spends less than she did!

She got sick for two weeks last year and seven stores closed in Scottsdale. (Use any city.)

She said to me, "I dreamt you bought me a new Mercedes."

I said, "In your next dream, drive it in good health."

She called me and said, "I have good news and bad news with the car."

I said, "Give me the bad news first."

She said, "I had an accident."

I asked, "What's the good news?"

She said, "The air bags work."

When she told me the car was stolen, I said, "Can you identify the thief?"

She answered, "No, but I did get the license plate number!"

When we first got married, we lived with my in-laws. Every time I wanted to make love to my wife, my mother-in-law would be knocking at our bedroom door. She yelled," What are you doing in there? What's going on? Leave my daughter alone!"

Finally, we couldn't take it any more. We went to an old cemetery about two blocks from the house. It was very quiet and no one was ever around. On nice nights we would go there, have a little wine, maybe a cigarette and make love.

One night when we got there, it was damp from a recent rain. I found a gravestone that had fallen over, and we sat down on it and proceeded to make love.

The next morning, my wife had a terrible backache. I rushed her to our family doctor. After examining her, he came out and said, "Gloria's back is going to be fine. But her ass died in 1847!"

CHAPTER 8

ETHNIC AND RELIGIOUS JOKES

Ethnic stories are a lot of fun. People of various backgrounds love to laugh at themselves. These jokes are also fun to tell because you can exaggerate the ethnic or religious mannerisms. People start laughing as soon as you start telling the story.

The first story is about a preacher in a small parish church in a little village in northern Scotland. The minister is delivering his sermon and asks, "Has anyone in the congregation ever seen a ghost?"

About half of the members stand up. He then asks, "Has anyone here ever touched a ghost?" Most of the people sit down. He then asks, "Has anyone here ever had sex with a ghost?"

Everyone sits down except old man McGregor. The minister looks at the old man and says, "Mr. McGregor, you're standing here in front of this congregation saying that you had sex with a ghost??!"

McGregor says, "A ghost? I thought you said 'a goat!!'"

It's Time to Get Up

Another ethnic story is about a mother going into her son's bedroom on a Saturday morning to wake him to tell him it was time to go to the synagogue.

He said, "I'm not going."

She asked, "Why not?"

He said, "I'll give you two good reasons. One, they don't like me and two, I don't like them."

His mother replies, "I'll give you two good reasons why you must go to the synagogue. One, you're fifty-four years old and two, you're the rabbi."

Irish Humor

Murphy

Into a Belfast pub comes Paddy Murphy, looking like he'd been run over by a train. His arm is in a sling, his nose broken, and his face cut and bruised.

"What happened to you?" asks Sean, the bartender.

"Jamie O'Conner and me had a fight," says Paddy.

"That little shit," says Sean, "He couldn't do that to you, he must have had something in his hand."

"That he did," says Paddy, "A shovel is what he had and he beat me pretty bad with it."

"Well," says Sean, "You should have defended yourself. Didn't you have anything in your hand?"

"That I did," said Paddy. "Mrs. O'Conner's breast, and a thing of beauty it was, but useless in a fight."

The Sleeping Scotsman

McDougal is walking along a field in Glengarry. After walking many miles, he gets a wee bit tired, so he sits down under a tree and falls asleep. After a while, two young lasses come strolling along and see old McDougal asleep under a tree.

One of the girls says, "You know, Mary, I've always wondered what a Scotsman really wears under his kilt."

Mary says, "Well, he's fast asleep, so let's take a peek."

They look under his kilt and start giggling. Mary says, "Why don't we leave a token of our visit."

She takes the blue ribbon out of her hair and ties it around old McDougal's pecker. They both run off laughing.

After a while, McDougal wakes up, stands up and says to himself, "Aye, it's time for a wee pee." When he looks down, he's stunned to see a blue ribbon tied around his yugger.

He says to himself, "I don't know where you've been and what you've done, but I'm glad to see you won first prize."

One For The Road

An Irishman who had too much to drink is driving home from the city one night and of course his car is weaving violently all over the road.

A cop pulls him over. "So," says the cop to the driver, "Where have you been?"

"Why, I've been to the pub," slurs the drunk.

"Well," says the cop, "it looks like you've had quite a few to drink this evening!"

"I did all right," the drunk says with a smile.

"Did you know that a few intersections back, your wife fell out of your car?" asks the cop.

"Oh, thank heavens," sighs the drunk. "For a minute there, I thought I'd gone deaf."

Shamus

Brenda O'Malley is home making dinner, as usual, when Tim Finnegan arrives at her door.

"Brenda, may I come in?" he asks. "I've something to tell you!"

"Of course you can come in. You're always welcome, Tim. Where's my husband?"

"That's what I'm here to be tellin' ya, Brenda. There was an accident down at the Guiness brewery..."

"Oh, God, no ... please don't tell me!" cries Brenda.

"I must, Brenda. Your husband Shamus is dead and gone. I'm sorry."

Finally, she looks up at Tim. "How did it happen, Tim?"

"It was terrible, Brenda. He fell into a vat of Guinness Stout and drowned."

Brenda replied, "Did he go quickly?"

"Well, no, Brenda. Fact is, he got out three times to pee."

Murphy

Murphy showed up at Mass one Sunday and the priest almost fell down when he saw him. Murphy had never been seen at church in his life.

After Mass, the priest caught Murphy and said, "Murphy, I am so glad you decided to come to Mass. What made you come?"

Murphy said, "I have to be honest with you, Father. A while back, I misplaced my hat and I really love that hat. I know that McGlynn had one just like mine and he came to church every Sunday. I also knew that McGlynn had to take his hat off during Mass and I figured he would leave it in the back of the church. So I was going to leave after Mass and steal McGlynn's hat."

The priest said, "Well, Murphy, I notice that you didn't steal McGlynn's hat. What changed your mind?"

Murphy said, "Well, after I heard your sermon on the Ten Commandments, I decided I didn't need to steal McGlynn's hat."

The priest gave Murphy a big smile and said, "After I talked about 'Thou Shalt Not Steal,' you decided you would rather do without your hat than burn in Hell, right?"

Murphy shook his head and said, "No, Father, after you talked about 'Thou Shalt Not Commit Adultery,' I remembered where I left my hat!"

The New Preacher

The new preacher is nervous about hearing confessions, so he asks the older preacher to sit in on his sessions. The new preacher hears a couple of confessions, then the old preacher asks him to step out of the confessional for a few suggestions.

The old preacher suggests, "Cross your arms over your chest and rub your chin with one hand. Now, try saying things like, 'I see, yes, go on, and I understand.'"

The new preacher tries these things. The old preacher says, "Now don't you think that's a little better than slapping your knee and saying, "No shit! What happened next?"

The First Time

A new priest at his first Mass was so nervous he could hardly speak. After Mass, he asked the monsignor how he had done.

The monsignor replied, "When I am worried about getting nervous on the pulpit, I put a glass of vodka next to the water glass. If I start to get nervous, I take a sip."

So the next Sunday, he took the monsignor's advice. At the beginning of the sermon, he got nervous and took a drink. He proceeded to talk up a storm. Upon his return to his office after Mass, he found the following note on the door:

1. Sip the vodka, don't gulp.
2. There are ten commandments, not twelve.
3. There are twelve disciples, not ten.
4. Jacob wagered his donkey, he did not bet his ass.
5. The Father, the Son and the Holy Ghost are not referred to as daddy, junior, and the spook.
6. David slew Goliath, he did not kick the shit out of him.

7. When David was hit by a rock and knocked off his donkey, don't say he was stoned off his ass.
8. We do not refer to the cross as the "big T."
9. Next Sunday, there will be a taffy pulling contest at St. Peter's, not a peter pulling contest at St. Taffy's.

Celibate

A young monk was assigned to an ancient monastery. His first job was to copy a very old copy of the Bible. He was told to do it in its original form. The monk worked for many days on this commission, but he was getting more and more frustrated every day.

The abbot noticed this and asked him, "What is the problem my son?"

The young monk replied, "Father, I hate to complain, but I have been making a copy of a copy. Do you not have the original?" It may be possible that the original copy of the Bible may have some mistakes and if I find them, they could be corrected."

The old abbot got very upset. He replied, "The original holy book is in the catacombs of this monastery and no one has looked at it in many years. I am sure there are no mistakes. In fact, it is almost inconceivable that there could be any."

But the young monk persisted and finally the old abbot agreed to read the ancient Bible. He said he would do it alone, as the book was very delicate and he was afraid that if anyone but himself touched it, it could be damaged. The old abbot went down into the catacombs and did not come up for many days.

The young monk was starting to be very concerned. He decided to go down into the catacombs to see if the old abbot was all right. As he descended the steps he heard someone weeping. Sitting at a table was the abbot.

The young monk approached and saw that he had the ancient Bible lying on the table in front of him. The young monk said to him, “Father, did you read the Holy Book?”

The abbot said, “Yes, my son!” As he continued crying, he said, “The word is ‘celebrate’!”

Know It All

A drunk who smelled of beer sat down on a subway seat next to a priest. The man’s tie was stained, his face was plastered with red lipstick and a half empty bottle of gin was sticking out of his torn coat pocket. He opened his newspaper and began reading.

After a few minutes the man turned to the priest and asked, “Tell me, Father, what causes arthritis?”

The priest replied, “My son, it is caused by loose living, being with cheap, wicked women, too much alcohol, sleeping around with prostitutes and a lack of personal hygiene.”

A minute later, the priest, thinking about what he said, put his hand gently on the man’s arm and apologized. “I’m sorry. I should not have come on so strong. How long have you had arthritis?”

“I don’t have arthritis, Father,” the drunk replied, “I was just reading in the newspaper that the Pope does.”

The Surgeon's Note

A nurse was on duty in the emergency room, when a young woman entered with purple hair styled in a punk rocker Mohawk. She was sporting a variety of tattoos and wearing strange clothing. It was quickly determined that the patient had acute appendicitis, so she was scheduled for immediate surgery.

When she was completely disrobed on the operating table, the staff noticed that her pubic hair had been dyed green, and above it there was a tattoo that read, "Keep off the grass." Once the surgery was completed, the surgeon wrote a short note on the patient's dressing gown, which said, "Sorry, had to mow the lawn."

Punishment

A young nun goes to the confessional. She's very nervous.

The priest says to her, "How can I help you, Sister?"

She replies, "I'm very upset, Father, for I have sinned."

The priest says, "Tell me about it."

The nun says, "Well, it's very hard to talk about."

The priest says, "Sister, this is a confession, cleanse your soul!"

She finally says, "Father, I am ashamed to tell you, but I don't wear panties under my habit."

"Is that it, my child?" The priest thinks for a moment, then says to her, "Sister, your punishment is to do three novenas, two hail Marys and three cartwheels."

The Drunk

A drunk happens upon a baptismal service on a Sunday afternoon down by the river. He proceeds to stumble down into the water and stands next to the minister.

The minister turns, notices the old drunk and says, "Mister, are you ready to find Jesus?"

The drunk looks back and says, "Yes, sir, I am."

The minister then dunks the fellow under the water and pulls him right back up. "Have you found Jesus?" the minister asks.

"No, I didn't!" says the drunk.

The minister then dunks him under for quite a bit longer, brings him up and says, "Now, brother, have you found Jesus?"

"No, I did not!" says the drunk again.

Disgusted, the minister holds the man under for at least 30 seconds this time, brings him up and demands, "For the grace of God, have you found Jesus yet?"

The old drunk wipes his eyes and pleads, "Are you sure this is where he fell in?"

Don't Take Tips

Two guys are at a race track. They're going to the pari-mutuel window when they happen to see two nuns collecting donations. They walk over to them and one of the guys says, "Hi, Sisters," and hands them $10 for their basket.

The Sisters thank them and the other guy says, "Sister, is it possible for you two to pick out a winning horse for us?" One of the nuns says, "Well, we never do any gambling, but since you were so nice to donate that money to us, we'll do it, but only this once. There is a horse running in the fifth race called 'Benedictus.'"

The guys thank the nuns and ran to the window to place their bet. When the race is over, their choice ran dead last. The guys are very upset and don't even look at the nuns when they pass.

One Sister turns to the other and says, "You know those two nice men who we gave that tip to speak Latin."

Sister Francis said, "Well, what did they say?"

So Sister Mary whispers, "They said, 'Benedictus fuctus'!"

———

The Candle

Mrs. Donovan was walking down the street one day in Dublin when she met up with Father Flaherty. The Father said, "Top of the morning to ye! Aren't ye Mrs. Donovan and didn't I marry ye and your husband a couple of years ago?"

She replied, "Aye, that you did."

The Father said, "Are there any wee ones yet?"

She replied, "No, not yet, Father!"

The Father said, "Well, I'm going to Rome next week and I'll light a candle for ye and your husband."

She replied, "Thank ye, Father."

Some years later, they meet on the street again.

The Father asked, "Well now, Mrs. Donovan, how are ye these days?"

She replied, "Very well, Father."

The Father asked, "Any wee ones, yet?"

She replied, "Oh yes, three sets of twins and four singles, ten in all!"

The Father said, "That's wonderful! How is yer loving husband doing?"

She replied, "Oh, he's gone to Rome to blow out your fooking candles!"

———

The Rabbi Convention

There's a rabbinical convention in Chicago. Rabbi Goldfarb is in his hotel room at 9 p.m. ready to retire for the night when there's a knock at the door. The rabbi says, "Who is it?"

He hears someone say, "special delivery." He opens the door and a beautiful, buxom young girl is standing there wearing a very short skirt.

The girl says, "I was sent by the men's club at your temple as a gift."

The rabbi is stunned but tells the girl to come in. He gets on the phone, calls the president of the men's club and says, "Sol, you have the nerve to send me a voman of the night?" He goes on berating Sol until the girl says, "Rabbi, I don't want to upset you so I'll go."

She gets up and gets ready to leave, but the rabbi says, "Oh, you can stay, it's not your fault."

———

Restricted

During the winter of 1926, Thelma Goldstein from Chicago treated herself to her first real vacation in Florida. Being unfamiliar with the area, she wandered into a restricted hotel in North Miami.

"Excuse me," she said to the manager. "My name is Mrs. Goldstein, and I'd like a small room for two weeks."

"I'm awfully sorry," he replied, "but all of our rooms are occupied."

Just as he said that, a man came down and checked out. "What luck," said Mrs. Goldstein. "Now there's a room."

"Not so fast, madame. I'm sorry, but this hotel is restricted. No Jews allowed."

"Jewish? Who's Jewish? I happen to be Catholic."

"I find that hard to believe. Let me ask you, who was the Son of God?"

"Jesus, son of Mary."

"Where was he born?"

"In a stable."

"And why was he born in a stable?"

"Because a schmuck like you wouldn't let a Jew rent a room in his hotel."

———

Catholic Nursing Home

A Jewish family is considering putting their grandfather in a nursing home. All the Jewish facilities are completely full so they have to put him in a Catholic home. After a few weeks in the Catholic facility they come to visit Grandpa.

"How do you like it here?" asks the grandson.

"It's wonderful. Everyone here is so courteous and respectful," says Grandpa.

"We're so happy for you. We were worried that this was the wrong place for you."

"Let me tell you about how wonderfully they treat the residents here," Grandpa says with a big smile. "There's a musician here—he's eighty-five years old. He hasn't played the violin in twenty years, and everyone still calls him 'maestro'! And there's a physician here—ninety years old. He hasn't been practicing medicine for twenty-five years and everyone still calls him 'doctor'!

"And me, I haven't had sex for thirty years and they still call me 'the fucking Jew.'"

———

You Gotta Be Jewish

A man walks into temple with a dog. The rabbi comes up to him and says, "Pardon me, this is a house of worship. You can't bring your dog in here."

"What do you mean," says the man. "This is a Jewish dog."

The rabbi looks carefully and sees that this dog has a tallis bag around its neck.

"Rover," says the man, "Daven!"

"Woof!" says the dog, who stands on his hind legs, opens the tallis bag, takes out a kipa and puts it on his head.

"Woof!" says the dog, who stands on his hind legs, opens the tallis bag, takes out a tallis and puts it round his neck.

"Woof!" says the dog, who stands on his hind legs, opens the tallis bag, takes out a holy book and starts to pray.

"That's fantastic!" says the rabbi. "It's absolutely amazing, incredible! You should take him to Hollywood, get him on television or get him in the movies. He could make a million dollars!!"

"You speak to him," says the man, "He wants to be a dentist."

The Sermon

A priest has just finished his morning sermon and is standing outside the church greeting his parishioners. A young woman walks by and the priest greets her. He says, "Good morning, my dear. Did you enjoy my sermon?"

She looks at him and says, "Go f—k yourself!"

The priest is stunned. He says, "How dare you speak to a man of the cloth like that. Do you realize that I may only be a priest now in a small neighborhood parish, but in five years, I could be an assistant bishop. In ten years, I could be a bishop. In fifteen years, I could be a cardinal. In twenty years, maybe even the pope!

"F—k Me? F—k you!"

Don't Take Any Chances

A man goes to see Mel Gibson's new movie, *The Passion of Christ*, and is inspired to take his family to Israel to see the places where Jesus lived and died.

While on vacation his mother-in-law dies. An undertaker in Tel Aviv explains that they can ship the body home to Wisconsin at a cost of $10,000, or the mother-in-law could be buried in Israel for US$500.

The man says, "We'll ship her home."

The undertaker asks, "Are you sure? That's an awfully big expense and we can do a very nice burial here."

The man says, "Look, 2,000 years ago they buried a guy here and three days later he rose from the dead. I just can't take that chance."

Akmed

Akmed came to the United States from Afghanistan. He was only here a few months when he became ill. He went to doctor after doctor, but none of them could help him. Finally, he went to an Arab doctor.

The doctor said, "Take dees bucket, go into the odder room, poop in de bucket, pee on de poop, and den put your head down over de bucket and breathe in the fumes for ten minutes."

Akmed took the bucket, went into the other room, pooped and peed on the poop, bent over and breathed in the fumes for ten minutes. He then returned to the doctor's office. He said, "It worked, I feel terrific! What was wrong with me?"

The doctor said, "You're homesick!"

Communing With Nature

Enjoying his stroll through the woods, a hiker comes up to another man hugging a tree with his ear firmly against the tree. Seeing this, the hiker inquires, "What the hell are you doing?"

The man replies, "I'm listening to the music of the tree!"

The hiker says, "You gotta be kidding me!"

The tree-hugger says, “Would you like to give it a try?”

So the hiker says, “OK.” He wraps his arms around the tree and presses his ear firmly against the tree.

In a flash, the other guy slaps a set of handcuffs on him, takes his wallet, jewelry, car keys, strips him naked, and leaves.

Two hours later, another nature lover strolls by, sees the guy handcuffed to the tree, stark naked, and asks, “What the hell happened to you?”

The hiker tells the guy the whole story about how he got there. The other guy shakes his head in sympathy, then walks around him, kisses him behind the ear and says, “This just ain’t your lucky day!”

The Best Tequila Ever

A Mexican is strolling down the street in Mexico City and kicks a bottle lying in the street. Suddenly out of the bottle appears a genie.

The Mexican is stunned and the genie says, “Hello, master. I will grant you one wish.”

The Mexican is thinking that he really likes drinking tequila and says, “I wish to drink tequila whenever I want, so make me piss tequila.”

The genie grants him his wish. When the Mexican gets home, he gets a glass and pisses in it. He looks at the glass and it’s clear. It looks like tequila. The he smells the liquid. It smells like tequila. So he tastes it and it’s the best tequila he ever tasted.

The Mexican yells to his wife, “Consuela, come quickly!”

She comes running down the hall and the Mexican takes another glass out and pisses into it. He tells her to drink it. Consuela is reluctant but takes a sip and says it is the best tequila she ever tasted. The two drink and party all night.

The next night, the Mexican comes home from work and tells his wife, "Consuela, get one glass out and we'll drink tequila."

The Mexican begins to piss in the glass and his wife says, "Pancho, why do we only need one glass?"

Pancho raises his glass and says, "Because tonight, my love, you drink from the bottle!"

Many Moons Later

I like Indian jokes. I also like Indians. I met an Indian girl once and took a chance on an Indian blanket.

Milton Berle

The Right Beat

General Custer couldn't stand what was happening at Little Bighorn. The night before, the Indians were so nice at the dance.

The battle was in full swing. The Indian drums kept up a steady beat. General Custer leaned over to his aide and said, "I don't like the sound of those drums."

From across the arroyo, an Indian chief yelled, "He's not our regular drummer!"

Indians have a new way of playing sex games. Instead of wife-swapping, they call it, "Passing the Buck."

Cochise, the great Indian chief, said to one of his braves, "Little Bull, if you masturbate, you will go blind."

Little Bull replied, "I'm over here, Chief."

Four Indian chiefs went into a restaurant for a bite. The maitre d' asked, "Do you have a reservation?"

One Indian chief answered, "Certainly. In Arizona!"

Milton Berle

Getting Lost

The great Indian chief, Falling Rocks, decided that his tribe would have to move to get food for the coming winter. He told them that he would leave and search the mountains and valleys for a place that the tribe would move to. He mounted his horse loaded with provisions and told his tribal leaders he would return before the full moon.

Many moons passed, and the tribal leaders became worried that something had happened to Falling Rocks. So they sent scouts out to search the mountains and valleys for their chief."

But to no avail. To this day the members of the tribe are still looking for him. In fact, you may still see signs that say, "Watch out for Falling Rocks."

Jack E. Leonard

What's In A Name?

A young Indian boy is walking with his father, Big Bear. He says, "Father, I have a question. How do Indians get their names?"

His father ponders for a moment, then takes his son by the hand and tells him to sit down. He then explains how Indians get their names.

"When your mother, Shooting Star, and I were first wed, we went down by the brook and made love. Nine months later, your sister, Babbling Brook was born.

"The next year, your mother and I made love under the tallest oak tree in the forest. Nine months later, your older brother was born and we named him Tallest Tree.

"Do you understand all of this, Broken Rubber?"

Little Bighorn

At the scene of the worst beating the 7th Cavalry ever experienced by the Sioux Indians at Little Bighorn, the United States government decided to build a monument at that site. An artist was hired and told that the government wanted a mural painted to depict the scene of the historic battle. They wanted the artist to capture Lt. Col. Custer's thoughts at the battle scene.

The artist painted the whole side of the monument to capture the feeling of the battle. Finally, the day arrived when the panorama would be unveiled. Hundreds of spectators and officials were there to witness the artist lifting the curtain to view the great panorama.

A gasp went up from the crowd. On the painting, there was the entire 7th Cavalry surrounded by thousands of naked Indians humping. The commissioner screamed at the artist, “How could you paint such a pornographic scene?”

The artist answered, “You wanted to show the battle scene and what Custer was thinking at the time, right?”

“That’s right,” yelled the commissioner, “but what does thousands of Indians screwing signify?”

The artist answered, “When Custer saw the Indian attack, he was stunned by the size of the hostile forces and yelled out, ‘Holy shit, look at all those fucking Indians.’”

The Don

An old Italian Mafia Don is dying and he calls in his grandson to his bedside. He says, “I wanna you lissena me. I wanna for you to taka my chrome-plated .38 revolver so you will always remember me.”

The grandson looks at him and says, “But Grandpa, I really don’t like guns. How about you leave me your Rolex watch instead?”

The old man says, “You lissena me. Somma day you gonna runna da business, you gonna have a beautiful wife, lotsa money, a bigga home and a couple of bambinos. Somma day you gonna come home and maybe finda you wife inna bed with another man!

“Whatta you gonna do then...pointa to your watch and say, times up?”

Two Friends

Two Italian men are walking along a street in Rome. Pietro says, “Hey, Giuseppe, I gotta ask you a question.”

Giuseppe says, "Okay."

Pietro asks, "Do you lika woman who has a bigga nose?"

Giuseppe says, "No!"

Pietro asks again, "You lika a woman who has a bigga wart on her face and hair under her arms?"

Giuseppe says, "Are you crazy? No!"

Pietro then asks, "Do you lika woman with a bigga fat ass and boobs that hang down?"

Giuseppe replies, "Why you ask these crazy questions?"

Pietro says, "I'm a gonna tell you. If you don't like those things I just asked you, then why you fucka my wife?"

The Deaf Bookkeeper

A Mafia Godfather finds out that his bookkeeper has screwed him for ten million bucks. This bookkeeper is deaf, and his deafness was considered an occupational benefit, and was why he got the job in the first place, since it was assumed that a deaf bookkeeper would not be able to hear anything he'd ever have to testify about in court.

When the Godfather goes to shake down the bookkeeper about his missing ten million bucks, he brings along his attorney, who knows sign language.

The Godfather asks the bookkeeper, "Where is the ten million bucks you embezzled from me?"

The attorney, using sign language, asks the bookkeeper where the ten million dollars is hidden.

The bookkeeper signs back, "I don't know what you are talking about."

The attorney tells the Godfather, "He says he doesn't know what you're talking about."

That's when the Godfather pulls out a 9-mm pistol, puts it to the bookkeeper's temple, cocks it, and says, "Ask him again!"

The attorney signs to the bookkeeper, "He'll kill you for sure if you don't tell him!"

The bookkeeper signs back, "OK! You win! The money is in a brown briefcase, buried behind the shed in my cousin Enzo's backyard in Queens!"

The Godfather asks the attorney, "Well, what'd he say?"

The attorney replies, "He says you don't have the balls to pull the trigger."

It's A Possibility

This little guy is in a public restroom taking a leak. Standing at the next stall is a huge man. The guy glances over at this huge guy and notices that he has the biggest male member he has ever seen.

The little guy says to the huge man, "I don't want to be presumptuous, but I have never seen a penis that size."

The big guy asks, "Are you coming onto me?"

The little guy says, "No! No! It's nothing like that. Do you mind if I ask you a question?"

The big guy is annoyed but says, "Okay, what's the question?"

The little guy says, "How did it ever get that big?"

The big man says, "Well, I put it in beans every day!"

The little guy then asks, "What kind of beans?"

The big guy replies, "Human beings!"

Another Urinal Story

Little Jake is standing at the urinal when another man steps up to the next stall. Jake looks at him and says, "I have never seen such a beautiful set of jewels in my life."

The man looks at Jake and says, "Are you crazy?"

Jake says, "Listen, if you let me touch your privates, I'll give you a hundred dollars."

The guy thinks it over. He can't believe a guy will give him $100 just to touch his joint. So he says, "Okay."

Then, Jake gets behind him, puts his hands on his thighs and grabs him right in his privates and says, "Alright, dis is a stick up!"

A One-Liner

The scariest words a man can hear in a public toilet? "Nice dick!"

You Came in Second

(told with a Yiddish accent)

Sadie tells Maurice, "You're a schmuck! You always were a schmuck and you always will be a schmuck!

"You look, act and dress like a schmuck! You'll be a schmuck until the day you die! And if they ran a world-wide competition for schmucks, you'd come in second."

"Why would I come in second?"

"Because you're a schmuck!" Sadie screams.

Do you know the difference between a bris (circumcision) and a divorce?

"In a divorce you get rid of the whole schmuck!"

Shooting Star

A young Jewish man calls his mother and says, "Mom, I'm bringing home a wonderful woman I want to marry. She's Native American and her name is Shooting Star."

"How nice," says his mother.

He says, "I have an Indian name, too. It's Standing Tall, and you will have to call me that from now on."

His mother says, "I have an Indian name, too. It's Sitting Shiva!"

Just Moved In

This old man is sitting on a bench at a Florida retirement community. A woman sits down next to him and says, "Are you new here?"

He replies, "Yes."

She says, "When did you move in?"

He says, "A few weeks ago."

She asks, "Where are you from?"

He says, "I've been around."

She says, "Yeah, but from where?"

He says, "Look, I'd rather not talk about it."

She says, "We're all friends here, you can tell me."

He says, "Well, I've been in the can!"

She says, "You've been in the toilet?"

He says, "No, not in the toilet, in jail."

She asks, "What did you do?"

He replies, "I murdered my wife, cut her up in little pieces and threw her body into the bay!"

The woman says, "Oh, so that means you're single?"

The Swim

Manny decides to go for an early morning swim at a Catskill mountain resort hotel that he's staying at. He walks down to the pool and sees an old man sitting on a rocker next to the pool.

He says, "Good morning, how's the pool?"

The old man says, "It's luk varm!"

So Manny takes off his robe and leaps into the pool. The water is so cold, he can hardly catch his breath!

He jumps out of the pool and says to the old man, "I thought you said the pool was lukewarm?"

The old man replies, "I didn't say dot. I said it looked varm!"

Advice

Schwartz is a very neurotic guy. He goes to the Chinese laundry to bring in his shirts to be laundered. Wong, the Chinaman, says to him, "You know, Mr. Schwartz, I know you a long time and you are always so nervous."

Schwartz says, "I know, but I can't help myself."

Wong says to him, "I tell you what to do and it will help you relax."

Schwartz says, "What should I do?"

Wong says, "You follow my instructions. First you go home, then you grab your wife, you take off her clothes, then you fill the tub with warm water, then you put her into the tub. Then you take her out and rub her with warm oil, then you powder her, throw her into bed and start to make love to her."

Wong continues to instruct Schwartz. "But then you stop. You take out a cigarette and have a little smoke. Then you start to make love again, you do this three or four times and you will become totally relaxed!"

Schwartz says, "All right, I'll do it."

He goes home, opens the door, grabs his wife, strips her and proceeds to give her a bath. She is stunned and says, "Jake, what the hell are you doing?"

Jake says, "Don't say a word!" He then rubs her down with warm oil, dries her, powders her and proceeds to make love to her. Then he stops, takes out a cigarette and lights up.

She says, "Jake, what are you doing?"

Jake says, "Don't rush me. ...I'm having a smoke."

He finishes his smoke then starts to make love again. He does this three times.

Finally, she says to him, "You know, Jake, you fuck just like a Chinaman."

He's Not Jewish

Sarah calls her mother from college. She says, "Mama, I have great news for you."

Mama says, "Yes Sarah, and what is the good news?"

Sarah says, "Well, I just got married."

"You got married?" says Mama.

Sarah says, "Yes, and he's really a nice boy. You and Poppa will love him."

After the mother calms down a little, she says, "So does he have a good job?"

Sarah answers, "Well, no, Mama, actually he isn't working right now, but he's looking."

Mama says, "Well, I guess he's young and it may take a little time for him to get a job. Where will you live?"

"Well, Mama, since he doesn't have a job we thought we could live with you and Poppa for a while," Sarah says.

"Well, I guess that could work out for a while," Mama says.

"One more thing, Mama, he's not Jewish!"

Mama says, "Oh, well, since you're married already, what can we do?"

Sarah says, "Mama, I thought perhaps we could sleep on the sofa bed in the living room."

Mama says, "Absolutely not! You will sleep in our bed in our bedroom."

Sarah says, "Mama, I can't take your bed."

Mama says, "Don't worry, Sarah, you can, because when I hang up, I'm gonna kill myself."

The Calendar

A Hebrew teacher stood in front of his class and said, "The Jewish people are observing their 5,765th year as a people. Consider that the Chinese, for example, have only observed their 4,695th year as a people. Now, what does that mean to you?"

After a moment of silence, a student raises his hand.

"Yes, Stanley," the teacher says. "What does it mean?"

Stanley replies, "It means that for 1,070 years, the Jews had to go without Chinese food."

The Wailing Wall

An old rabbi visited the Wailing Wall to pray, twice a day, for several years. In an effort to check out the story, CNN sends a reporter, who watches the bearded old man at the wall praying.

When he turns to leave, she approaches him for an interview. After she introduces herself, she asks, "How long have you been coming to the Wailing Wall to pray?"

"For about fifty years," he informs her.

The reporter then asks, "What do you pray for?"

"I pray for peace between the Jews and Arabs. I pray for all the hatred to stop, and I pray for all our children to grow up in friendship."

The reporter asks him how he felt after doing this for fifty years.

"Ahh, it's like talking to a wall!"

Pick A Winner

A young Jewish man excitedly tells his mother that he's fallen in love and is planning to get married, adding, "Just for fun, Ma, I'm going to bring over three women and you try to guess which one I'm marrying."

The mother agrees. The next day, he brings three beautiful women into the house, seats them on the couch and they chat for a while. He then says, "Okay, Ma, guess which one I'm going to marry."

She immediately says, "The one on the right!"

The young man says, "That's amazing, Ma. You're right! How did you know?"

The mother replies, "She's the one I didn't like."

A Wonderful Family

In a small town, in the old country, the rabbi died. His widow was so disconsolate that the people of the town decided that she should get married again. The town was so small that the only eligible bachelor was the town butcher. The poor widow was dismayed because she'd been wed to a scholar and the butcher had no formal education.

However, she agreed and they were married. After the marriage, on Friday night, the woman proceeded to light candles. The butcher leaned over to her and said, "My mother told me that before lighting the candles, it's a mitzvah to have sex." So they did.

Then, she lit the candles. He leaned over to her again and said, "My father told me that after lighting the candles, it's good to have sex." So they did.

The next morning, when they awoke, he said to her, "My grandmother said that before you go to temple, its a mitzvah to have sex." So they did.

After praying all day, they came home to rest, and again he whispers in her ear, "My grandfather says after praying, it's a mitzvah to have sex." So they did.

On Sunday, she went out to shop for food and met a friend who asked, "So, how is your new husband?"

She replied, "Well, he's no scholar, but he comes from a wonderful family."

Hadassah

Four Jewish women—all members of Hadassah (a charitable organization)—were riding in a Caddy convertible. Out of nowhere, a truck crashed into them and they were killed instantly.

After three days, God asked his angel, Gabriel, to find the four Hadassah women and not to come back without them. So Gabriel spread his wings and went in search of the women. He searched everywhere but one place, Hell!

Finally, he went there and confronted the Devil. The Devil said, "Of course they are here! They got here by mistake."

Gabriel said, "I have come to take them back to Heaven!"

The Devil said, "You can't have them!"

Gabriel said, "Why not?"

The Devil said, "Because they've been here only three days and already they've raised $100,000 for air conditioning!"

The Jewish Dog

A guy goes to his rabbi and says, "Rabbi, I have a request. We have a pet dog that is going to be thirteen years old and we love the dog and want to have it bar mitzvahed!"

The rabbi is in shock and says, "You have the nerve to come before me and ask me to bar mitzvah your dog?"

The guy says, "Listen, Rabbi, I didn't want to upset you so I'll just take the $25,000 that I was going to donate to the temple and give it to another charity."

The Rabbi says, "Wait a minute, why didn't you tell me the dog was Jewish?"

The Hobby

Morris and Abe are sitting on a park bench in Miami Beach, talking about trivial things and how they're getting older.

Abe says, "You know, Morris, ve should get involved in something to keep us busy.

Morris says, "Like vhat?"

Abe says, "How about some kind of hobby?"

Morris replies, "I have a hobby already."

Abe says, "You have a hobby? Vat kind hobby you got?"

Morris says, "I keep bees."

Abe asks, "So vere do you keep the bees?"

Morris replies, "I keep them in my condo."

Abe asks, "Vere in the condo do you keep the bees?"

Morris answers, "In the closet."

Abe asks, "You keep the bees in the closet? Aren't you afraid dey'll sting Rose ven she opens the closet door?"

Morris says, "I keep them in a plastic bag."

Abe asks, "You keep the bees in a plastic bag? Vouldn't dey suffocate and die?"

Morris says, "Dey vould...but who gives a shit! It's only a hobby."

Wrongly Done

Every Monday, for the past twenty-five years, Goldberg would take his beloved tallis (prayer shawl) to Ginsberg's Dry Cleaners to be pressed and ready for the Sabbath.

Every Friday, Goldberg would pick up his newly pressed tallis and pay $10 for the pressing.

One Monday, Goldberg walks into Ginsberg's Dry Cleaners with his tallis and sees a few Oriental people working behind the counter. Seeing a surprised look on Goldberg's face, Mr. Wong explains that he has recently purchased the store.

Goldberg then tells Wong that for the past twenty-five years he has been coming into the store every Friday to bring his tallis in to be pressed and then he picks it up every Monday. He makes sure to tell Wong that he has been charged $10 for the service all those years.

Wong says, "No probrem, we keep same price. You be happy customer."

So Goldberg leaves his tallis there to be pressed. When he comes back on Monday to pick it up, it's all wrapped and ready for him. Then he's presented with the bill. Instead of the usual $10 bill, the bill says $20.

Goldberg looks at the bill and gets very upset. He says to Wong, "You said that you would keep the same price that Ginsberg always charged."

Wong says, "We try, but it take us over three hours to take knots out of fringes."

Sadie and Yetta

Sadie and Yetta were talking. Sadie says, "That nice Morris Finkleman asked me out for a date. I know you went out with him last week and I wanted to talk to you before I give him an answer."

Yetta says, "Vell...I'll tell you. He shows up at mine apartment very punctual. He is wearing a nice suit. He brought me beautiful flowers. Then he takes me downstairs, takes me in a beautiful car out for dinner. We have a marvelous dinner, then he takes me to a show.

"I really enjoyed myself. So then, we come back to mine apartment and he turns into an animal. He becomes completely crazy and tears off my expensive dress and has his way with me!"

Sadie asks, "Oh! So you are telling me that I shouldn't go out with him?"

To which Yetta replies, "No, I'm just saying that if you go, be sure to wear a cheap dress!"

Schwartz

A mortician was working late one night, as it was his job to examine the bodies before they were sent off to be buried. As he examined the body of Mr. Schwartz, he made an amazing discovery. Mr. Schwartz had the longest private part he had ever seen!

"I'm sorry, Mr. Schwartz," said the mortician, "but I can't send you off to be buried with a huge private part like this. It has to be saved for posterity."

The mortician used his instruments to remove the dead man's member, stuffed his prize into a briefcase and took it home with the intention that he would bring it to the museum in the morning.

The first person he showed it to was his wife. "I have something to show you that you won't believe," he said and opened his briefcase.

His wife looked in the briefcase and screamed, "Omigod, Schwartz is dead!"

The Shabbos

The rabbi has just finished the Saturday service and is outside the temple waiting to greet all the members as they leave the temple. As three men pass by, he stops them and says, "Bernie, Dave, Saul! I would like to ask a question of all of you. What would you consider a good Shabbos?"

Bernie says, "Well, to me, a good Shabbos is getting up early, getting dressed, putting on my running suit, and going for a 5-mile run. Then, I take a nice shower, have breakfast with the family, go to temple and when I come home, have dinner with the family."

The rabbi says, "That's a good Shabbos, Bernie! What about you, Dave?"

Dave replies, "Well, I also get up early. I go to the store, get the paper, come back, have a nice breakfast with the kids and my wife. Then I read the paper, go to temple, return home, take the kids to the park and go out to dinner with my wife."

The rabbi agrees, "David! That's a very nice way to spend a Shabbos. What about you, Saul?"

Saul replies, "Well, I get up very early. I have breakfast, get dressed and go for a walk. On the way back to my house, I stop at my girlfriend's house, go in, get undressed and proceed to make love. Then I take a shower, get dressed and go to the temple. On the way back home, I stop at my girlfriend's house again. I get undressed. We take a shower together, get into the bed. I shtup her for about an hour, then get up and take another shower. I get dressed, go home and have dinner with my family."

The rabbi and the other two guys look at Saul, speechless! Finally, the rabbi says to him (raising his voice), "You stand there and have the nerve to tell me that's a good Shabbos? No! No! No! That's not a good Shabbos. That's a great Shabbos!"

The First Jewish President

The first Jewish President calls his mother on the phone in Brooklyn, New York. He says, "Hello, how are you, Momma? This is Joseph. I have great news for you. I'm throwing a huge party here at the White House in a couple of weeks and would like you to come."

His mother says, "It's nice of you to ask, Joseph, but who do I know there? What would I do? I'd feel uncomfortable there."

The president says, "Momma, what are you talking about? I want all the dignitaries to meet you. It would be an honor for me. I'll send my private plane, Air Force One with my personal pilot, Colonel Roberts.

"Then, my special limo with my personal chauffeur will pick you up and take you directly to the airport. When you land in Washington, a special car will be waiting and take you to the White House.

"After the party, I will have you taken back to the airport and fly you back to New York on Air Force One. A car will then take you back to your home in Brooklyn."

Finally, after much persuasion, she agrees to go. When the time comes, she packs her suitcase, has the porter bring it down to the front of the house where she waits for the limo to pick her up.

While she's waiting, her neighbor, Mrs. Goldberg, walks by and says, "Sadie, it looks like you're going on a trip?"

Sadie says, "I am!"

Mrs. Goldberg questions her, "So where are you going? Is it to anyone I know?"

Sadie answers, "Well, you know my son, the doctor? I'm going to see his brother!"

A Dining Experience

A fleeing Taliban, desperate for water, was plodding through the Afghanistan desert when he saw something far off in the distance. Hoping to find water, he walked towards the image, only to find a little old Jewish man sitting at a card table with a bunch of neckties laid out on it.

The Arab asked, "I'm dying of thirst, can I have some water?"

The Jew replied, "I don't have any water, but why don't you buy a tie? They are only $150. Here's one that goes very nicely with your robes."

The Arab shouted, "I don't want an overpriced tie, you idiot, I need water!"

The Jew replied, "OK then, don't buy my ties. But to show you what a nice guy I am, I'll tell you that over that hill there, about four miles away, is a nice restaurant. Walk that way; they have all the water you need."

The Arab grudgingly thanked him, then staggered away towards the hill and eventually disappeared. Four hours later the Arab came crawling back to where the Jewish man was sitting behind his card table.

The Jew said, "I told you, about four miles over that hill. Couldn't you find it?"

The Arab rasped, "I found it all right. Your brother wouldn't let me in without a tie."

Italian Cookies

An elderly Italian man lay dying in his bed. While suffering the agonies of impending death, he suddenly smelled the aroma of his favorite Italian anisette sprinkled cookies wafting up the stairs. He gathered his remaining strength and lifted himself from the bed.

Leaning against the wall, he slowly made his way out of the bedroom, and with even greater effort, gripping the railing with both hands, he crawled downstairs. With labored breath, he leaned against the door frame, gazing into the kitchen.

Were it not for death's agony, he would have thought himself already in Heaven, for there, spread out upon waxed paper on the kitchen table were literally hundreds of his favorite anisette sprinkled cookies. Was it Heaven? Or was it one final act of heroic love from his devoted Italian wife of sixty years, seeing to it that he left this world a happy man?

Mustering one great final effort, he threw himself towards the table, landing on his knees in a crumpled posture. His dry lips parted, the wondrous taste of the cookie already in his mouth, seemingly bringing him back to life.

His aged and withered hand trembled on its way to a cookie at the edge of the table when it was suddenly smacked with a spatula by his wife.

"Back off!" she said, "They're for the funeral."

The Confession

A parish priest was being honored at a dinner on the twenty-fifth anniversary of his arrival in that parish. A leading local politician, who was a member of the congregation, was chosen to make the presentation and give a little speech at the dinner, but he was delayed in traffic, so the priest decided to say his own few words while they waited.

"You understand," he said, "the seal of the confessional can never be broken. However, I got my first impressions of the parish from the first confession I heard here. I can only hint vaguely about this, but when I came here twenty-five years ago I thought I had been assigned to a terrible place.

"The very first chap who entered my confessional told me how he had stolen a television set, and when stopped by the police, had almost murdered the officer. Further, he told me he had embezzled money from his place of business and had an affair with his boss's wife.

"I was appalled. But as the days went on I knew that my people were not all like that, and I had indeed come to a fine parish full of understanding and loving people."

Just as the priest finished his talk, the politician arrived full of apologies at being late. He immediately began to make the presentation and give his talk.

"I'll never forget the first day our parish priest arrived in this parish," said the politician. "In fact, I had the honor of being the first one to go to him for confession."

A Nosh

These two old guys were talking. Sam says, "You know, I went out with a great gal the other night. We went out for a few drinks, then went to her apartment. We had a few more drinks, got undressed and jumped into the sack. It was amazing! She sprayed whipped cream on my pecker, then put a cherry on it!"

His friend says, "Then what happened?"

Sam replied, "Then she ate it! What an experience! Would you like me to arrange a date with her for you?"

His friend said, "Sure." So, his friend goes out with her and then meets Sam the following day.

Sam said, "So, what happened?"

His friend said, "Well, we went out, had a few drinks, then went back to her place. We got naked, then she put cream cheese and lox on my dick."

Sam said, "So, what happened then?"

His friend said, "Well, it looked so good, I ate it myself!"

An Old Man Story

Two old guys were talking about their girlfriends. Stan says, "I had a wonderful time with Trudy last night."

His friend says, "What did you do?"

Stan says, "Well, we went out for a nice dinner, then we went back to her place, got undressed and got into bed."

His friend says, "Then what did you do?"

Stan continues, "Well, I started singing 'Strangers In The Night,' and then we fell asleep."

His friend says, "Tonight, I'm going out with Harriett and I'm gonna do the same thing."

So they meet a few days later and Stan says, "So, how was your date the other night?"

His friend says, "Well, we went to dinner, went back to her place, got undressed and got into bed. Then I started to sing to her 'Strangers In The Night' just like you did."

Stan said, "So, then what happened?"

His friend said, "Well, I forgot the words to 'Strangers in the Night,' so I fucked her!"

We Love Our Kids

An elderly man in Miami calls his son in California and says, "I hate to ruin your day, but I have to tell you that your mother and I are divorcing. Forty-five years of misery is enough."

"Pop, what are you talking about?" the son screams.

"We can't stand the sight of each other any longer," the old man says. "We're sick of each other, and I'm sick of talking about this, so you call your sister in Chicago and tell her," and he hangs up.

Frantic, the son calls his sister, who explodes on the phone, "Like heck they're getting divorced," she shouts. "I'll take care of this."

She calls her father immediately and screams at the old man, "You are NOT getting divorced! Don't do a single thing until I get there. I'm calling my brother back and we'll both be there tomorrow. Until then, don't do a thing, DO YOU HEAR ME?" and hangs up.

The old man hangs up his phone and turns to his wife. "Okay," he says, "They're coming for Rosh Hashana and paying their own airfares."

"Now what do we do for Passover?"

Dencing

A young Orthodox Jewish couple are getting married. The future bridegroom goes to see his rabbi. He says, "Rabbi, I have a question. I know our custom prohibits me from dancing with my wife at our wedding, but could you waive that rule?"

The rabbi says, "No way, ve have to obey the rituals! No dencing is allowed betveen man and woman."

The young man says, "Well, what about having sex before the ceremony? There's a little room in the back—we could do it there!"

The rabbi says, "It's a very small room."

The young man says, "Well, we can do it standing!"

The rabbi gets all excited and says, "You can't do dat...No, no, no!"

The young man says, "Why not?"

The rabbi says, "Because it could lead to dencing!"

The Commitment

Mr. Nichols gets a call from the Brotherhood at his temple. He picks up the phone and says, "Hello!"

The temple member says, "You made a pledge of $10,000 at the last meeting of the Brotherhood. When can we expect the check?"

Mr. Nichols says, "I'm not giving it to you!"

The member says, "Mr. Nichols, at the last meeting at the temple, you stood up before all the temple members and made a commitment."

Mr. Nichols says, "That's right! I know what I said and I know what a commitment is! A commitment is when you have an eighty-five-year-old mother and have to put her in a retirement home that costs $30,000 a year. That's a commitment! A commitment is when you have a brother who lost $50,000 at the race track and if he doesn't pay, the bookies will break his legs! That's a commitment! A commitment is when you have a kid who has to go to college for four years at $40,000 a year! That's a commitment."

"You're right," says the member. "So what's the problem?"

"I wouldn't give to them, so why should I give to you?"

Business Practices

A man has been in business for many, many years and the business is going down the drain. He is seriously contemplating suicide and he doesn't know what to do. He goes to his rabbi and tells him about all of his business problems, and asks the rabbi what he should do.

The rabbi says, “Take a beach chair and a Bible, put them in your car, take them to the ocean and sit on the beach. The wind will riffle the pages for awhile and eventually the Bible will stay open at a particular page. Read the first words your eyes fall on and they will tell you what to do.”

The man does as he is told. He places the beach chair at the water’s edge and opened the Bible. The wind riffles the pages of the Bible, which stop at a particular page. He looks down at the Bible and his eyes fall upon the words that tell him what he has to do.

Three months later, the man and his family come back to see the rabbi. What a change! The man is wearing a $1,000 silk suit. The wife is all decked out in a fur coat and the child is dressed in a beautiful silk outfit.

The man hands the rabbi a thick envelope full of money and tells him he wants to donate the money to the temple in order to thank the rabbi for his wonderful advice.

The rabbi is delighted. He thanks the man and asks him what words in the Bible brought this good fortune to him.

The man replies, “CHAPTER 11.”

The Traveler

A man arrives in Ben Gurion International Airport in Tel Aviv with two large bags. The customs agent opens the first bag and finds it full of money in different currencies. The agent asks the passenger, “How did you get this money?”

The man says, “You will not believe it, but I traveled all over Europe going into public restrooms. Each time I saw a man pee, I grabbed his penis and said, 'Donate money to Israel or I will cut your balls off.'"

The customs agent said, "Well, it's a very interesting story. What do you have in the other bag?"

The man answered, "You would not believe how many people in Europe do not support Israel."

The Provider

A young woman brings home her fiancé to meet her parents. After dinner, her mother tells her father to find out about the young man. The father invites the fiancé to his study for a drink. Then, he asks, "What do you do for a living, young man?"

"I am a Torah scholar," he replies.

"A Torah scholar. Hmmm," the father says. "Very admirable, but what will you do to provide a nice house for my daughter?"

"Don't worry, sir, God will provide," replies the young scholar. The conversation proceeds like this, and each time the father asks questions, the young idealist insists that "God will provide."

Later, his wife asks, "So, what do you think, Honey?"

The father answers, "He has no job and no plans, but the good news is he thinks I'm God."

The Rowing Team

There was an article in the sports section of the New York Times a few weeks ago. It seems Yeshiva University in the Bronx announced the first rowing team in the history of the school. So I went up to see what was going on. I managed to meet the rabbi, who also was the coach of the team.

I said to the rabbi, "How come you decided to field a rowing team?"

"Vell," he said, "The boys need more than just religion. They have to learn to compete in the outside world. In fact, they have their first match next week against Harvard."

I said, "Harvard has one of the best college rowing teams."

The rabbi replied, "I know! However, we might be able to win because we have determination and the will to win!"

I said to him, "I'd like to come back and get the results." He said it wasn't a problem!

So, the following week, I went and met with the rabbi. I was very curious to find out how Yeshiva did. I said, "So, Rabbi, how did the boys do?"

The rabbi said, "Vell, not bad! Of course, we lost, but not because Harvard had a better team."

I asked, "Then why?"

The rabbi answered, "Vell, it's simple. Harvard has eight rowers and one talker."

The Jewish Samurai

There once was a powerful Japanese emperor who needed a new chief samurai. So he sent out a declaration throughout the entire known world that he was searching for a chief.

A year passed, and only three people applied for the very demanding position: a Japanese samurai, a Chinese samurai, and a Jewish samurai.

The emperor asked the Japanese samurai to come in and demonstrate why he should be the chief samurai. The Japanese samurai opened a matchbox, and out popped a bumblebee.

Whoosh! went his sword. The bumblebee dropped dead, chopped in half.

The emperor exclaimed, "That is very impressive!"

The emperor then issued the same challenge to the Chinese samurai—to come in and demonstrate why he should be chosen.

The Chinese samurai also opened a matchbox and out buzzed a fly. Whoosh, whoosh, whoosh, whoosh! The fly dropped dead, chopped into four small pieces.

The emperor exclaimed, "That is very impressive!"

Now the emperor turned to the Jewish samurai, and asked him to demonstrate why he should be the chief samurai. The Jewish samurai opened a matchbox, and out flew a gnat. His flashing sword went whoosh! But the gnat was still alive and flying around.

The emperor, obviously disappointed, said, "Very ambitious, but why is that gnat not dead?"

The Jewish samurai just smiled and said, "Circumcision is not meant to kill."

The Easy Way Out

A man went to see the rabbi. "Rabbi, something terrible is happening and I have to talk to you about it."

The rabbi asked, "What's wrong?"

The man replied, "My wife is poisoning me."

The rabbi, very surprised, asked, "How can that be?"

The man then pleaded, "I'm telling you, I'm certain she's poisoning me. What should I do?"

The rabbi then offered, "Tell you what. Let me talk to her. I'll see what I can find out and I'll let you know."

A week later, the rabbi calls the man and says, "Well, I spoke to your wife for three hours. You want my advice?"

The man said yes, and the rabbi replied, "Take the poison."

Outer Space

A man is driving down a highway in Arizona when a beautiful woman appears out of nowhere right in front of him...completely nude...and with green skin.

Stunned, he starts to speak to her. "Excuse me, but you just popped out of thin air. How did you do that?"

"Oh," says the woman, "I'm from Andromeda, in what you call outer space."

"Andromeda?" says the man, "Wow! Do all the women on Andromeda have green skin like yours?"

"Yes," replies the woman, "everyone is green on Andromeda."

The man continues to stare. Then, he says, "Excuse me for asking, but I can't help but noticing that you have twelve toes on each foot. Here on Earth we all have five toes on each foot. Do all Andromedans have twelve toes on each foot?"

"Yes, they do," replies the woman.

"And forgive me for saying this, but it's hard not to notice," the man continues. "You have three breasts. Do all Andromedan women have three breasts?"

"Yes," replies the woman, "Actually, everyone on Andromeda has three breasts."

"Please, may I ask you one more question?"

The woman nods.

"I also can't help noticing that on each of your hands you have seven fingers and on each finger is a very large diamond. Here on Earth diamonds are very rare and valuable. Do all Andromedan women have diamonds on seven fingers of both hands?"

"Well," the woman answers, "not the shiksas."

A Jewish woman is sitting at a bar. A man approaches her.

"Hi, honey," he says. "Want a little company?"

"Why?" asks the woman. "Do you have one to sell?"

The Visit

Becky's grandson and his wife are coming to visit her for the first time. So she's giving him the directions to her flat.

"You come to the front door of the Golfers Greenblock of flats. I am in flat number 32 on the 14th floor. At the front door, you'll see a big panel of buttons. With your elbow push button 32. I will buzz you in. Then come inside, the lift is on the right. Get in, and with your elbow hit 14. When you get out, I am on the left. With your elbow, hit my doorbell."

"Grandma, that sounds easy, but why am I hitting all these buttons with my elbow?"

"You're coming empty-handed?"

It was mealtime during a flight on El-Al.

"Would you like dinner?" the flight attendant asked Moshe, seated in first class.

"What are my choices?" Moshe asked.

"Yes or no," she replied.

An elderly Jewish man is knocked down by a car and brought to the local hospital. A pretty nurse tucks him into bed and says, "Mr. Epstein, are you comfortable?"

Epstein replies, "I make a nice living...."

Saul Epstein was taking an oral exam, applying for his citizenship papers. He was asked to spell "cultivate" and he spelled it correctly. He was then asked to use the word in a sentence, and with a big smile, responded, "Last vinter on a very cold day, I vas vaiting for a bus, but it vas too cultivate so I took the subvay home."

Jewish Optimism

A story is told of a Jewish man who was riding on the subway reading an Arab newspaper.

A friend of his, who happened to be riding in the same subway car, noticed this strange phenomenon.

Very upset, he approached the newspaper reader: "Moshe, have you lost your mind? Why are you reading an Arab newspaper?"

Moshe replied, "I used to read the Jewish newspaper, but what did I find? Jews being persecuted, Israel being attacked, Jews disappearing through assimilation. So I switched to the Arab newspaper. Now what do I find? Jews own all the banks, Jews control the media, Jews are all rich and powerful, Jews rule the world. The news is so much better!"

———

More Schtick

A rabbi was opening his mail one morning. Taking a single sheet of paper from an envelope, he found written on it only one word: "schmuck."

At the next Friday night service, the rabbi announced, "I have known many people who have written letters and forgot to sign their names, but this week I received a letter from someone who signed his name...and forgot to write a letter."

———

Three Jewish women get together for lunch. As they are being seated in the restaurant, one takes a deep breath and gives a long, slow "oy." The second takes a deep breath as well and lets out a long, slow "oy." The third takes a deep breath and says impatiently, "Girls, I thought we agreed that we weren't going to talk about our children."

———

Signs on synagogue bulletin boards:

- Under same management for over 5,763 years.
- Don't give up. Moses was once a basket case!
- What part of "Thou shalt not" don't you understand?

Chanukah songs that never quite caught on:

- Oy to the World
- Schlepping through a Winter Wonderland
- Matzo Man (by the Lower East Side Village People)
- Come on Baby, Light my Menorah
- Deck the Halls with Balls of Matzos
- Silent Night? I Should Be So Lucky

CHAPTER 9

FLYING STORIES

Years ago, I was afraid to fly. The first time I flew, I went on a trip to Mexico. I walked into the lobby of the airline terminal and I saw a sign on a metal showcase selling travel insurance. It was very expensive and I figured if the terminal was so dangerous, air travel would be astronomical and really dangerous.

I went to an army surplus store and told the clerk that I was going on a dangerous trip and had to fly over water. I didn't want to tell him that I was afraid to fly. He told me to buy shark repellent and a 2-foot floating knife. At least, if we crashed over the Gulf of Mexico, I'd be prepared.

The airline fares were very expensive so I decided to fly on a "no-frills" airline. They didn't sell tickets, they sold chances. All the planes have a bathroom and a chapel.

There is no movie—you don't need one. Your whole life keeps flashing before your eyes!

Captain Hans von Schmidt, a pilot on Lufthansa Airlines, made this announcement on a subsequent trip to Europe that I was on:

"We are having difficulty with our engines and we have to ditch the plane. When we hit the water, all the business class passengers, please step out on the right wing. All the first class passengers step out on the left wing. A launch will pick up all the first class and business class passengers shortly. The rest of the passengers, remain in your seats, and of course, thank you for flying Lufthansa."

The Flying Dream (a true story)

I have had a recurring dream over the years that I can fly. No, not on a plane, I feel that I'm flying all by myself. In the dream, I'm in a crowded room. I run a few steps and start to lift off in a vertical position. I then move to a horizontal position and I'm in flight. I'm not soaring, just sort of floating in a very large room. There are many people in the room. I look down at the people and they are all applauding and I'm euphoric.

That is the recurring dream, but this particular dream is a little different.

The beginning of the dream was the same as all the others, but after the people start to applaud, I start to tell jokes. When I look up, I see a platform about eight feet high and decide I will fly up to the platform and tell the jokes from there so I could have a better view of the audience.

I was still dreaming when I threw my right leg up in the air and pushed my body as hard as I could, to lift off! The next thing I knew, I was on the floor! My wife woke up, looked down, saw me on the floor and said, "What happened?'

I replied that I dreamt I was flying and actually started to take off when I fell on the floor.

She said, "Flying, are you nuts?"

I said, "I guess I must have run out of gas!" When I fell, I missed the night stand by an inch.

She said, "From now on, when you go to sleep I will have to strap you in with a belt!"

Now, things have calmed down. I'm thinking of getting a bigger house with a larger bedroom. I'll build a longer runway for takeoffs and I'll only plan scheduled flights!

Questions and Answers

A mother and her young, inquisitive son were flying Southwest Airlines from Kansas City to Chicago. The son, who had been looking out the window, turned to his mother and asked, "If dogs have baby dogs and cats have baby cats, why don't planes have baby planes?"

The mother (who couldn't think of an answer) told her son to ask the flight attendant. So the boy dutifully asked the flight attendant, "If dogs have baby dogs and cats have baby cats, why don't planes have baby planes?"

The flight attendant responded, "Did your mother tell you to ask me that?"

The little boy admitted that she did.

"Well, then, tell your mother that there are no baby planes because Southwest always pulls out on time. Now, let your mother explain that to you."

---

73 Ain't That Old

Two elderly Wal-Mart greeters were sitting on a bench during break time and one turns to the other asking, "Slim, I'm seventy-three years old and I'm just full of aches and pains. I know you are about my age. How do you feel?"

Slim says, "I feel just like a newborn babe."

Rather amazed, his coworker repeats his statement in the form of a question, "Really? A newborn babe?"

"Yup," grins Slim. "No teeth, no hair and I think I just wet my pants."

What's In A Name

A man boards an airplane and takes his seat. As he settles in, he glances up and and sees the most beautiful woman boarding the plane. He soon realizes that she is heading straight to the seat next to him. She sits down and fastens her seat belt.

He says to her, "So where are you flying today?"

She turns and smiles and says, "To the annual Nymphomaniac Convention in Chicago!"

He swallows hard and is instantly crazed with excitement. Struggling to maintain his cool, he calmly asks, "What's your role at the convention?"

She answers, "Well, I try to debunk some of the popular myths about sexuality!"

He says, "Really, what myths are those?"

"Well, she explains, "one popular myth is that African-American men are the most well endowed, when it is a known fact that the Native American is most likely to possess this trait. Another popular myth is that Frenchmen are the best lovers, when it is actually men of Jewish descent who romance women the best!"

The man replies, "Very interesting!"

Suddenly, the woman becomes very embarrassed. She says, "I'm sorry, but I feel so awkward discussing this with you and I don't even know your name!"

The man, smiling, extends his hand and replies, "Tonto. Tonto Goldstein!"

The Note

A businessman is flying to New York when he notices the man across the aisle is sleeping but he is unaware that his fly is open and his package is showing. He doesn't want to call the flight attendant because he doesn't want to embarrass the passenger.

So he decides to write him a note. He does this, gets up from his seat, leans over and taps the sleeping passenger. As the man opens his eyes, the well-meaning businessman hands him the note.

It says, "Hi! My name is Bruce Philips. I'm sitting across the aisle from you. I didn't want to call attention to the fact that your fly is open and your privates are showing! P.S. I love you!"

Copilots

A plane leaves Los Angeles Airport under the control of a Jewish captain. His copilot is Chinese. It's the first time they've flown together and an awkward silence between the two seems to indicate a mutual dislike.

Once they reach cruising altitude, the Jewish captain activates the autopilot, leans back in his seat, and mutters, "I don't like Chinese."

"No rike Chinese?" asks the copilot, "Why not?"

"You people bombed Pearl Harbor, that's why!"

"No, no," the copilot protests, "Chinese not bomb Peahl Hahbah! That Japanese, not Chinese."

"Japanese, Chinese, Vietnamese...doesn't matter, you're all alike!"

There are a few minutes of silence.

"No rike Jews!" the copilot suddenly announces.

"Why not?" asks the captain.

"Jews sink Titanic."

"Jews didn't sink the Titanic!" exclaims the captain, "It was an iceberg!"

"Iceberg, Goldberg, Greenberg, Rosenberg, no mattah...all same."

The Old Pilot

A ragged-looking older man shuffled into a bar. Stinking of whiskey and cigarettes, his hands shook as he took the "Piano Player Wanted" sign from the window and gave it to the bartender.

"I'd like to apply for the job," he said.

The bartender wasn't too sure about this doubtful-looking old guy, but it had been a while since he had a piano player and business was falling off. "What do you do?" he asked.

"I used to be a fighter pilot. I flew several hundred combat sorties in 'Nam, among other things," was the answer.

The bartender decided to give him a try, as he really needed more business. "The piano is over there...give it a go."

The man staggered over to the piano and several patrons snickered. By the time he was into the third bar of music, every voice was silenced. What followed was a rhapsody of sound and music unlike anything anyone had ever heard in the bar before. When he finished, there wasn't a dry eye in the place.

The bartender bought the guy a beer and said that he sounded very good. He asked, "What do you call that tune?"

The man said, "It's called 'Drop Your Panties, Baby, We're Gonna Rock and Roll Tonight,'" and he took a long pull of the beer.

"I got another one," and he began to play again. What followed was a knee-slappin' bit of ragtime that had the place jumping. People were coming in from the streets to hear this guy play.

After he finished, the pilot acknowledged the applause and told the crowd that last song was called "Big Boobs Make My Afterburner Dance."

He then excused himself as he went off to the men's room. After thinking a bit, the bartender decided to hire the guy, no matter how bad he looked, or whatever he called his songs.

When the guy came out of the men's room, the bartender went over to tell him that he had the job, but noticed the old pilot's fly was undone and his member was hanging out.

He said "The job is yours but first I got to ask, do you know your fly is undone and your pecker is hanging out?"

"Do I know it?" The pilot replied, "Hell, I wrote it!"

A Flying Story

Mr. Rosenberg, a middle-aged man, is sitting in a window seat on a plane going to Israel. Just before takeoff, a large Arab wearing a beautiful caftan walks down the aisle and sits down next to him.

For a while, everything seems OK, but Rosenberg has to go to the restroom and he doesn't want to bother the Arab, who is sleeping. He figures he'll just wait until the Arab gets up.

But the Arab keeps snoring away and Rosenberg starts to feel more and more uncomfortable. After a while he's feeling nauseous as well. He tries to hold it in, but then AAARRGGHH—he throws up all over the Arab and the beautiful garment he's wearing.

Rosenberg thinks to himself, when the Arab wakes up, he'll kill me.

Finally, the Arab wakes up and sees the vomit all over him. Mr. Rosenberg looks at him and says, "Well, do you feel better now?"

Trouble in the Air

There was an airplane going down and the pilot got on the intercom and said, "If we get rid of some extra weight, we may be able to make it." They threw off all of the luggage, but they were still going down.

The pilot got on the intercom again and said, "Unfortunately, we're going to have to start by throwing out people. To be fair, we will go in alphabetical order by race, so when we call you, please step forward and jump out of the plane.

"We will start with 'A': African Americans." Nobody moved.

"All right, then, 'B': Blacks." Again, nobody moved.

"C': Colored people." Still nobody moved.

Her little boy asked, "Why aren't we moving?"

She said, "Honey, today we're Shvartzas."

CHAPTER 10

ANIMAL STORIES

Molly and Me

My wife and I took my granddaughter to Sky Harbor International Airport when she was going to camp for two weeks. We also took our fluffy little white Bichon, Molly, with us.

Every time I take my pup anywhere, women stop to pet and talk to her. Molly goes absolutely nuts. She wants to kiss them and lick them. She lays on her back so they can rub her belly. It's a sight to behold.

They never even take the smallest notice of me. I could be invisible. I really don't mind the lack of attention but I think to myself I should have owned a dog forty years ago. Dogs are like a magnet. Every woman who walks by Molly either smiles at her or wants to touch her.

I really love my little animal. I bought her from a breeder six years ago. My granddaughter was nine years old at the time and pestered us for over a year. I mean, she begged, cried, cajoled and finally drove me to a shrink. After all her begging and whining, we agreed to purchase the dog.

My granddaughter promised she would walk the dog every day after school. She also promised she would brush the pup's fur and brush her teeth daily. We kept a record of her reaction to her responsibilities.

In the six years since we got the dog, she walked her approximately six times. That was after threatening to send her to Siberia—in time for the annual famine, if she didn't walk the dog. I must admit that she does brush her teeth. Of course, this is for a fee that must be paid in dollars to her at the very moment she finishes brushing.

I'm sure this sounds familiar to families who have pets. The famous words I've heard from most everyone I tell this story to is, kids promise everything but never deliver. That's kids for you.

Think of this scenario! Why can't humans greet each other the same way as we greet animals. For instance, if I see an attractive woman standing with another person (it could be a man or woman), I approach her and I direct my question to her companion.

I could say, "Hi! Would it be all right to pet your lady? How about me giving her a lick and would you mind if she lays down on her back so I can rub her belly? Also, would you mind if I took her home with me and would it be all right if I hump her leg?"

You can picture the results. You would either be arrested or put away in an asylum, but wouldn't it be fun just to give it a try?

Well, I have to walk Molly now and then give her a bath and brush her teeth. My granddaughter doesn't have the time. She's at the shopping mall!

The Doberman

A man is mowing his lawn on a peaceful Sunday morning. He happens to glance up at his roof, and sees some movement behind the chimney. He stops the mower, looks up, and to his surprise, a large gorilla sticks his head out from behind the chimney.

The homeowner quickly takes out his cell phone and calls the zoo. He says, "Are you missing a gorilla?"

The zookeeper is very excited and says, "Yes! Yes! Have you seen him?"

The homeowner says, "I think he's on the roof of my house."

The zookeeper says, "Give me your address and don't do anything to provoke the animal and I'll be there in a few minutes."

In less than ten minutes, a white van pulls up and the zookeeper jumps out of the van and says, "Where's the gorilla?"

The homeowner points to the roof and they both see it. The zookeeper says, "I want you to follow my instructions." He runs to the van and comes back with an assortment of different items. He has a big net, a shotgun, and a ferocious looking Doberman sitting in the van.

He says, "Listen carefully, this is what we are going to do. I'm going up on the roof. I'm gonna get behind the gorilla and kick him off the roof. When he hits the ground, he will be stunned and at that time, you throw the net over him. The Doberman will come charging out of the van and bite the gorilla right in his yugger, immobilizing him. You got it?"

The homeowner nods, but the zookeeper says, "Wait. Repeat it to me once so I know you understand."

The homeowner says, "All right, you go up on the roof. Then you get behind the gorilla and kick him off the roof."

The zookeeper nods. "Right. When he hits the ground he will be stunned. At that time, you throw the net over him and the Doberman will come flying out of the van and bite the gorilla right in his privates, totally immobilizing him. You got it!?"

The homeowner says, "Yeah!"

As the zookeeper starts to go up on the roof, the guy says, "I have one question!"

Getting very annoyed, the zookeeper says, "What is it?"

The homeowner asks, "What do I do with the shotgun?"

The zookeeper says, "If the gorilla kicks me off the roof, SHOOT THE DOBERMAN!"

Surprise Ending

Two second and third grade elementary school teachers decide to take their classes to the race track to see the thoroughbred horses. They take all the students to the paddock to watch the horses run. It's very exciting for the kids.

After a while, the kids start getting restless and want to go to the bathroom. One of the teachers says to the other, "I'll take the girls to the ladies' restroom and you take the boys to the men's restroom."

The other teacher says, "I can't go into the men's room!"

The first teacher says, "Then let them go into the bathroom by themselves; it will be okay."

So she sends the little boys into the bathroom. They're in the bathroom ten seconds when all the boys come running out, very upset. The teacher asks what's wrong.

The boys say, "The urinal is too high and we can't reach it."

The teacher says, "Calm down." She looks into the men's restroom, sees no one is in there, and tells the boys she will go in with them and help them.

She picks up the first boy to help him reach the urinal, and then the second boy. When she picks up the third boy, she happens to glance down and sees that he is very well endowed.

She asks, "Are you in the third grade?"

He looks back at her and says, "No, lady, I'm riding Seabiscuit in the fifth, but thanks for the lift!!!"

Deepest, Darkest Africa

Three natives are standing around talking. One of them says, "I just came from the deepest part of the jungle and I saw the most ferocious animal that I have ever seen. It had wings that were ten feet wide and claws that were bigger than a lion's. It came swooping out of the trees and was the most ferocious animal that I ever saw!"

The other native says, "Ha! I have seen the most ferocious animal. This one came charging out of the desert and destroyed everything in its path. It had teeth as big as a man's hand. It had a head bigger than a hippo and it screamed as it attacked. That was truly the most ferocious animal I have ever seen!"

The third native says, "You call that ferocious? I saw the most ferocious, meanest animal. It was called the Poo Cat. It had a head on top and a head on the bottom!"

One of the other natives says, "Wait a minute. You're telling me that this animal had a head on top and a head on the bottom?"

The third native says, "Yes, that's what I'm saying."

"Well," says the other native, "If he had a head on top and a head on the bottom, how does he shit?"

The third native says, "He doesn't. That's what makes him so ferocious!"

The Porcupine

An elderly gentleman was walking through the London Zoo. He stopped at the porcupine cage. He called over the zoo attendant and asked, "Young man, do North American porcupines have larger pricks that the ones from Africa?"

The attendant thought for a moment and replied, "Well sir, the African porcupine's quills are sharper, but their pricks are the samc size!"

The Bullfrog

A woman goes into a pet shop. She wants to have a pet to keep her company. She asks the salesman if he would recommend a suitable pet for her. He says, "I have a wonderful pet for you. It's unusual as far as pets go but I know you would love it."

She says, "What kind of pet is it?"

He takes her over to a cage, and in the cage, sitting on a rock, is this large bullfrog.

She says, "You gotta be kidding me!"

The salesman says, "This is a special frog. You take it home, get undressed, get into bed, put the frog between your legs and just lay back and enjoy. Lady, if you don't think this is the best sex you ever had, I'll take the frog back!"

She finally agrees, goes home, gets undressed, gets into bed, puts the frog between her legs and waits for him to do his stuff. The frog just lays there and doesn't move. Finally, after an hour of waiting with nothing happening, she gets up, calls the pet shop and tells off the salesman.

He says, "I can't understand it, that frog has always performed. I'll be right over." When he gets to her house, he says, "Show me what you did."

So she lays down, spreads her legs and put the frog there. The frog does nothing. She says, "See, he doesn't do a damn thing!"

The guy grabs the frog and says, "This is it, I'm gonna show you what to do one last time!"

Big Shot

This takes place at a pet clinic. This small spaniel is sitting in the corner looking very unhappy.

This Great Dane walks over and says, "What's the matter, pal?"

The spaniel says, "Well, I'm very upset."

The Great Dane says, "Why?"

The spaniel says, "Well, the other day when my mistress was putting her stockings on, I went over to her and started humping on her leg."

The Great Dane says, "So what happened?"

The spaniel says, "Well, that's why I'm here. They're gonna castrate me. What about you?"

The Great Dane says, "Well, my mistress was bending over putting a roast in the oven. So, as she was bending over, her skirt went up, I got a little excited and jumped on her backside."

The spaniel says, "Wow, are they gonna cut your balls off, too?"

The Great Dane replied, "Nah!" (holding one of his big paws out). "I'm just here to have my nails done."

Eating Good

Things are not going well for Irving, so he has to cut expenses. He tells his wife, Myrna, that he heard dog food is very healthy and half the price of regular food.

His wife says to him, "You're crazy if you think I'm going to eat dog food."

He says, "Well, I'm going to try it!" So he goes to the pet shop and buys twelve cans of dog food.

He goes home, opens a can and eats the dog food. He says, "Honey, it's not bad! In fact, it's quite tasty."

Irving proceeds to eat it on a regular basis for over a week. Meanwhile, Irving's sister calls, speaks to Myrna, and asks how Irving is. Myrna says that he's been eating dog food and he loves it. Irving's sister want to speak to him and Myrna says, "You can't, because he's in the hospital."

His sister asks, "What happened to him?"

Myrna replies, "Well, he was on the kitchen table, licking his balls, when he fell off and broke his neck!"

Talking Dog

A man sees a sign in front of a house, "Talking Dog for Sale." He rings the bell and the owner tells him the dog is in the back yard. The guy goes into the back yard and sees the mutt.

"You talk?" he asks.

"Yep," the mutt replies.

"So, what's your story?" asks the guy.

The mutt looks up and says, "Well, I discovered I had this gift very young and I wanted to help the government, so I told the CIA about my gift and in no time, they had me jetting from country to country, sitting in rooms with spies and world leaders, because no one figured a dog would be eavesdropping. I was one of the most valuable spies for eight years. The jetting around really tired me out and I wanted to settle down. So, I signed up for a job at the airport to do some undercover security work, mostly wandering near suspicious characters and listening in. I uncovered some incredible dealings and now I'm retired."

The guy is amazed. He goes back in and asks the owner what he wants for the dog.

The owner says, "Ten dollars."

The guy says he'll buy him, but asks the owner, "This dog is amazing. Why on earth are you selling him?"

The owner replies, "He's such a fucking liar."

The Zebra

In an attempt to domesticate a zebra, the zoo people take her to a farm to introduce her to the farm animals. The zebra is happy to be let loose. She walks up to a pig and says, "What do you do around here?"

The pig says, "Well, they use me for ham and bacon." Then, the zebra walks over to some sheep and asks the same question.

The head sheep says, "Well, we get sheared for our wool."

The zebra then skips over to a large bull grazing on the grass. She says, "I'm new around here but what do you do around here?"

The bull slowly looks the zebra up and down and says, "Take off those pajamas and I'll show you what I do around here."

Not One Call

An Englishwoman is on a safari through Kenya. After hiking for many hours through the jungle, the group decides to pitch camp. Nature calls and the woman has to pee. As she is pulling up her trousers afterwards, a huge gorilla leaps out of the underbrush, rips off her clothes, and proceeds to have sex with her.

The woman is too paralyzed with fear to yell out. When the big ape finishes her off, he throws back her clothes and scampers off into the jungle.

The woman barely manages to put her clothes back on, and stumbles back into camp. All of the group surrounds her asking where has she been.

The woman doesn't utter a word. She just looks around and collapses. When she awakens many hours later in a hospital in Johannesburg, South Africa, she is practically comatose. For days she doesn't communicate with any of the doctors or nurses.

Finally, her mother comes from England to visit her. Her mother says, "Darling, I know you have been through a very harrowing experience, being sexually abused by a wild animal. But look at the upside. He could have killed you! Now you must put on your best English demeanor, a stiff upper lip and face the world."

Her daughter looks at her mother and finally after two weeks of silence, she starts to talk.

Her mother says, "Now, that's better."

Her daughter says, "You don't understand, Mummy. He hasn't called, e-mailed, or written in over three weeks."

Same Gorilla, Different Victim

Two gay guys are walking through a zoo. They come across the gorillas and notice that the male gorilla has a massive erection. The gay men are fascinated by this. One of the men just can't bear it any longer, and he reaches into the cage to touch it. The gorilla grabs him, drags him into the cage and mates with him for six hours nonstop, while the zoo attendants helplessly stand by.

When he's done, the gorilla throws the man out of the cage. An ambulance is called and the man is taken away to the hospital. A few days later, his friend visits him in the hospital and asks, "Are you hurt?"

"AM I HURT? "he shouts. "Wouldn't you be? He hasn't called. ...He hasn't written...."

Parrot Stories

This guy has two female parrots and keeps them in a large cage. He has a major problem with them. Whenever he brings a woman to his apartment, the parrots screech in the most vile language: "Nice boobs on that broad," "we're prostitutes," "big ass," and so on!

The guy can't take it any more, so he goes back to the pet shop and explains the situation. He says to the owner, "Unless something can be done about their cursing, I'm getting rid of them."

The owner of the shop says, "Listen, I have two male parrots who are great. They are calm and very religious. They are always praying. Why don't you take these two males and put them in the cage with the females. Maybe they will have a good influence on them."

So the man takes the two male parrots home and puts them in the cage with the females. The females start screeching, "We're prostitutes," etc. and all kinds of sexual insinuations.

Meanwhile, the two religious male parrots are praying. Finally, the two parrots look at each other and one of them whispers to the other one, "See, I told you our prayers would be answered!"

Jesus is Watching You

A thief is robbing a house. He goes into the living room and is filling his bag with all kinds of stuff. All of a sudden he hears a voice, "Jesus is watching you!"

He thinks maybe he's hearing things and continues to put stuff in his bag. He hears the voice again, "Jesus is watching you!" He shines a flashlight in the corner of the room and there is a big cage with a parrot in it.

The crook says, "Are you telling me something?" The parrot replies, "Jesus is watching you!"

The thief starts to laugh and says, "Are you Jesus?"

The parrot says, "No, Jesus is the big pit bull in the corner!"

Chapter 11

WESTWARD, OH!

There are always a lot of stories about living in California. Here are some of the funnier ones that I've heard.

Everyone in California is in therapy. It's a good thing they don't have parking spaces for the emotionally handicapped. There would be no place to park!

There are three million interesting people in New York and ninety-five in Los Angeles!

When I first moved here, I realized this is the only place where you wake up in the morning to the sound of birds coughing!

The only difference between California and yogurt is that yogurt has an active culture!

I heard about the the Mercedes back-to-school sale in Beverly Hills!

An intellectual in Hollywood is anyone who can read freeway signs without moving his lips!

California is a nice place to live—if you happen to be an orange!

The Casa Loma Hotel: Only in Hollywood

We moved to Los Angeles in 1979. I decided to get out of New York at that time because I couldn't deal with the snow and sleet.

That year, I was stuck in the city for over a week. There was a tremendous blizzard and the commuter trains weren't running so commuters couldn't get home.

I was lucky to have a friend who had an apartment on 86th Street and 3rd Avenue, right in the heart of the city. The storm was so bad, people actually were cross-country skiing on Park Avenue.

I called my wife and told her, "That's it! We're out of here." Later that year, we sold our house on Long Island and moved to California.

One of the first things we did was to open a small showroom on Grand Avenue in downtown Los Angeles. The name of my display company in New York City was Trimco. So we opened a western division and called it Trimco West.

The showroom wasn't in the most desirable section of town. Our showroom was a single story building with a front door that had a metal screen in front of it. The metal screen didn't keep the homeless people from sleeping in front of the gate, but since I was from New York and had worked in Manhattan, it was very common to experience this kind of situation.

Almost every morning when we arrived there, I would gently nudge the bums to wake them up. If they didn't respond to my nudging, I would then drag them to the bus stop and help them onto the bench for waiting bus passengers. I was hoping somehow they would gather enough strength to crawl onto one of the city buses.

Seeing homeless people was nothing new to me. In fact, when I was younger, I didn't mind dating homeless women. When I took them home after being out with them for the evening, I could drop them anywhere.

When we first arrived in Los Angeles, we found a small condo in Pacific Palisades. It was beautiful there. The condo was only a five minute drive from Santa Monica Beach and located on the famous Sunset Boulevard. Wherever we drove, film makers were making movies or shooting television sit-coms. Cameras were everywhere. I was in heaven.

I fantasized about being discovered. Sometimes standing in the crowd, I imagined someone would shout to me, "Hey, fella! Our star didn't show up, go over to makeup and get ready to step into his role."

Yeah, it was a dream, but you never know.

I traveled back and forth to my company's main headquarters in New York City once a month. I was bi-coastal but I told people at that time that I was also bisexual. When I wanted sex, I had to buy it!

One morning when I was in New York City, I phoned my wife to see how things were going at the showroom. I said, "Hi, honey. What's happening back home?"

She was all excited. She said, "You wouldn't believe what's going on across the street at the Casa Loma Hotel." (The Casa Loma was a dilapidated little hotel.)

She continued, "The SWAT team has the place surrounded and the police are using megaphones to warn the people inside to throw down their weapons and surrender. This is going to be an exciting movie. I haven't seen any of the stars yet because there is so much smoke!"

I said to my wife, "Honey, do you see any cameras or camera crews?"

She answered, "No…"

I continued, "Do you see any director chairs or lighting booms?"

She again answered, "No…"

I said, "Do you see any makeup people?"

She said, "No..."

So I said, "Then get your ass out of there right now! That hotel is being surrounded and is under siege for real."

She seemed dumbfounded. Then she said, "Oh my God, you're right. We're leaving right now. The Casa Loma is being surrounded by police."

I laughed for two days after that episode. Thank God, everything worked out and no one was hurt.

California Dreaming

California has a beacon light that seems to call many millions of people to resettle there. In fact, some people say that if you tipped the United States toward the west coast, all the oddballs would end up in California.

Moving out there was very exciting—it was the land of dreams and celluloid. I passed many famous people on the street and said to myself after I walked past them, "Hey! I know that person."

"Excuse me, sir, don't I know you?" I'd say.

The usual reply was, "I don't think so."

The next question was, "Are you from New York?"

The usual reply was, "Yes I am, but I really don't think we know each other."

I usually asked, "What's your name?"

The actor I met at the time answered, "Robert De Niro."

My usual reply was, "Oh, I knew I'd seen you before. Sorry about that."

He said, "No problem," and we both continued on our separate ways.

It's amazing how many times that happened. It's hard to place the faces when they are out of their environment.

My move to California was similar to Moses wandering in the desert for forty years. Of course, I only wandered in California for eighteen years. As my show business aspirations started to wane, I was busy working at my day job in order to support my family.

I had to travel back to New York City every two or three weeks, which didn't make it easy to get involved with comedy or acting. I did manage a few roasts for friends to keep my hand in the arena.

Things seemed to stay pretty static for me while we lived in California. I really can't complain, though. The weather was almost always perfect and I loved the casual lifestyle.

I did manage to connect with the Fontaine Modeling Agency only because friends of mine, Judy and Steve Ellis, owned the agency. They called me to go on a cattle call (that's when almost every agency sends their people out to audition for a job).

I found it very degrading to have to wait and wait and wait until some little twerp called my name, handed me a piece of paper and said, "Read it!"

One day, I was sent to an audition in Santa Monica on a hot Sunday morning in July to read for the part of a pizza salesman with an Italian accent. He had to be able to play golf.

That day, we were invited to the wedding of my godson. I got to the audition on time, at about 9 a.m. There were at least seventy or eighty guys already waiting there. The audition was held at the Holiday Inn near the beach in Santa Monica. Everyone was standing or sitting around the outdoor pool.

The temperature was quickly rising and everyone seemed to have a sullen attitude. The people who were running the audition were working out of one of the suites just off the pool area.

The actors would go into the audition room. When they left, very few of them were smiling. After waiting for close to two hours, I was really getting pissed off. No one offered us any water or a timetable as to when we would be called. Finally, I said to myself, "This is real bullshit."

I had to leave shortly to get to the wedding so I decided to go to the audition room door and knock to find out when I would be called. But when I knocked, no one answered.

I knocked again. Finally after about five minutes, the door opened and a young man, probably in his thirties, said to me, "What the fuck do you want?"

I was taken aback by his rude behavior but I held my temper and said, "My name is Buddy Stein and I would appreciate if you could tell me what time I'll be called in for my audition."

He looked at me for a minute, as if I were an alien from outer space, and said, "You'll do the audition when I call you. Now get back with the group." He then slammed the door in my face. There was complete silence as forty or more guys stared at me.

I looked at them and said to myself, "Okay." I again knocked on the door very forcefully. In a few seconds the door opened and the same guy (who turned out to be the director) looked at me and said, "I thought I told you to wait until you are called."

I didn't answer him, but instead I grabbed him by the throat and pulled him out of the room. With our faces inches apart I said, "Listen, you poor excuse for a human being, I asked you a simple question, you piece of turd, and I expect a reasonable reply."

He couldn't move, as I had him in a hold that was taught to me by a kung fu instructor Jyn Cho Hi (a famous Korean master of that art). He struggled in vain as I pushed him toward the pool. The crowd was stunned into silence as I said to the little creep, "Learn to respect the people who need this work."

After saying that, I pushed him head first, clothes and all into the pool. The crowd erupted in applause. When the creep surfaced, I said to him, "I just retired from show business, you little bastard." (Of course, I was kidding).

I walked to the exit feeling pretty good. I never bothered to find out what the director's name was, but I hope he treated people with a lot more empathy.

A Good Story

Rachel, the daughter of a very Orthodox Jewish family, comes home one night and says to her parents, "I have to tell you something that's very important!"

Her father said, "So, vat is it?"

She says, "Momma and Poppa, I'm getting married to the most wonderful man!"

The mother says, "You're getting married? Who is he?"

"Well, Momma, don't be upset but he's an Indian!"

Her mother says, "An Indian? Vat are you talking about?"

Rachel says, "Well, he's a wonderful person. He's a Native American from the Arapaho tribe and his name is Broken Arrow."

The father goes bananas! He says, "Don't talk to me! I don't want to see you any more. Leave us in our misery." And he walks out of the room.

The mother is hysterical and Rachel leaves and marries Broken Arrow.

A few years later, not having spoken to her parents in all that time, she makes a night call to her family. Her mother answers the phone. Rachel says, "Momma, it's Rachel!"

The mother says, "Rachel, how are you? We've missed you!"

Rachel says, "Momma, I'm fine and I have wonderful news for you! Put Poppa on the phone. Momma, please tell him it's very important that he pick up the extension."

Reluctantly, he does so.

Rachel continues, "Poppa, I have wonderful news for you."

He says, "So, vats the vonderful news?"

Rachel tells him, "Poppa, you have a grandson! I know how unhappy you were when I married Broken Arrow, but you have a grandson now and Broken Arrow has agreed to give our child a Jewish name!"

So the father says, "Well, I guess after all these years and since you're giving our grandchild a Jewish name, it will be okay! So tell me, Rachel, what is his name?"

Rachel says, "Whitefish!"

I always loved that joke. It actually came in handy one day while living in Los Angeles. Because we had to do extensive traveling for business, we decided to have a security system installed in our home. The day the installation was completed, we were scheduled to leave on an extensive buying trip abroad.

The installer said, "Please give me a few numbers for the code and a password that you will remember."

Since we were telling the whitefish joke so often, we decided to use "whitefish" as our password. So we told the installer that would be our password.

We left for several weeks right after that, and when we returned, with so many things on our minds, we both totally forgot the code and the password. We arrived at our home, put the key in the lock and opened the door. It tripped the alarm! We had forgotten the code!

We both racked our brains to remember the numeric code and finally did, but the security company called to check up on why the alarm went off. We remembered the password had something to do with a fish...a Jewish fish....

The security company called and asked, "Is everything OK there?" I said, "Yes."

The man on the phone said, "Then what is your password?"

I said, "Lox?" The man said, "No!"

I said, "Oh, that's right...it's whitefish!"

He said, "Okay!" After we wiped the sweat off our brows, we chuckled and never forgot our code again!

The Idolmaker

Prior to our move to California, my cousin, Gene Kirkwood (aka Gene Stein), became a big-time Hollywood producer. Gene grew up in New Rochelle, New York and babysat for our sons when they were young. When Gene was eighteen, he went to Hollywood to go into movies. He acted in a few films that weren't blockbusters, but hit it big after he produced the first *Rocky* film with Sylvester Stallone, who wrote the screenplay and rocketed to stardom.

We lost contact with him until we moved to Los Angeles. Shortly after our arrival, I contacted Gene. He seemed very happy to hear from me after so many years and invited us to his home. He told me all about his future plans.

I was very impressed with the Hollywood scene. I felt this is where I belonged, in the heart of the entertainment world. We saw Gene on several occasions but I was frustrated because I wanted to be a professional entertainer.

When we visited with him, we talked about a new film that he was going to produce. It was called, *The Idolmaker*. It was the story of a frustrated singer who couldn't make it in show business, but discovers and then becomes personal manager to two young singers. He controls their lives and molds them into rock 'n roll singers.

The story was loosely based on the story of Bob Marcucci, who created the two teen idols, Frankie Avalon and Fabian. The movie starred Ray Sharkey, who was a fine actor. Unfortunately, he passed away at a very young age.

I thought to myself, this would be a good chance to get into a movie. So I asked Gene to give me a part in the film. Actually, I begged, and after hours of groveling, I finally wore him down. He told me that there might be a small part for me at the end of the movie. He would send me the script and we would discuss my part after I read the script.

I received the script and was thrilled. I couldn't believe that I finally would be in a full-length feature film. I told every person I knew in the world about the film. I even told people I never met.

I used to walk down a street, stop people and say, "Hi, I'm going to be in a movie called *The Idolmaker!*" Many people actually ran away from me!

When I asked Gene what my part would be, he said, "In the last five minutes of the movie, in a nightclub scene, the two singers have become famous and they are entertaining there. Your part will be as a stand-up night club comic. You will have to do three minutes of comedy and then introduce the guys."

I worked on my three-minute monologue with a passion. I slaved for hours every day trying to make every word that came out of my mouth a gem. I couldn't sleep and my regular job was forgotten.

I was driving my wife nuts. I don't know how she put up with me. I was such a basket case that I was already writing my acceptance speech for a supporting actor performance at the Academy Awards. I was finally ready, so bring on the cameras!

Without a warning, a bolt out of the blue, the roof caved in! Gene called me and said, "Buddy, I have bad news for you." I thought someone in the family had died.

He continued, "Buddy, as you know, I hired Taylor Hackford to direct the movie. Taylor is a fine director and has directed many movies. He reviewed your part, decided the part was superfluous and didn't want to introduce another character."

I was so stunned, I could hardly breathe. Finally, I managed to say, "Are you nuts? What can I tell all the people who are looking forward to seeing me in a film? Who the f—k is Taylor Hackford? You're putting up all the money, tell him to go and screw himself."

Gene said, "Well, I'm paying this guy a lot of money. It's his call and I won't change it."

I was crushed. I made up a cockamamie story that the film ran over budget and they had to cut out my scene. The film opened to mild reviews. I always think that if my part was left in, it would have been a blockbuster.

I haven't see Gene for many years. There are no hard feelings. We just drifted apart and except for a very few members of my family, we don't stay in contact with each other. I don't even know if my parents are still alive!" (only kidding)

The Big Quake!

There were a lot of little incidents over the next few years while we lived in California, but nothing having to do with show business. It was an enjoyable experience until that early morning wakeup call on January 17, 1994 at 4:30 a.m.

That's when the Northridge earthquake hit in all its fury. We were sleeping at the time. Many people who did not live in Los Angeles asked me, "What did it feel like?"

I thought a freight train had gotten lost and was going through our bedroom at a tremendous speed. I yelled at my wife, "I'm going to get Alexis" (our granddaughter, who lives with us and was five years old at the time). As I stood up, it felt like a giant hand grabbed me and then threw me fifteen feet across the room into a wall.

Gloria (my darling wife) yelled that Alexis was already in our bed. She had come in ten minutes before the quake hit. It seemed like an eternity of rocking and rolling in our house. In reality, it shook us up for about twenty-five seconds. All the electricity stopped and everything was totally black. The only thing we could hear were sirens.

We all got up and stood in the doorway of our bedroom for about twenty minutes until the shaking had subsided. We were totally shook up. I found a flashlight and we got dressed and went downstairs. I remembered that we had an earthquake survival kit in my car in the garage.

After a few minutes, the aftershocks started. Gloria and Alexis were petrified and I was just scared. It was a very helpless feeling. I finally opened the trunk of my car and quickly opened the kit that had sat in my car for at least two years.

I found the batteries for the flashlight in the kit. They didn't work. We weren't hungry, so we didn't even bother to open up the survival food package. The water in the other packages had dried up and the mini-shovel was nowhere to be found.

People always ask me what they should do in case of an earthquake. I tell them, "Don't panic and stand inside the frame of a door. Then put your head between your legs and kiss your ass goodbye! Because it's all over!"

We ran into the street. People brought out sleeping bags and blankets and said they were too afraid to go back inside their homes. Two of our neighbors packed up their cars and left. I felt like doing the same.

So we did! About two days later, we decided to leave Los Angeles, since my wife and granddaughter could not fall asleep due to the aftershocks. They both tried to sleep on the couches in the living room. Gloria slept in her running suit and sneakers, along with a shovel, flashlight and a knapsack filled with emergency provisions. One little shake and she was out of there.

I asked her, "What about us?"

She said, "If it starts rocking, I'm taking the money and you're on your own."

The next day we left for Phoenix.

CHAPTER 12

MY FAVORITE ONE-LINERS AND QUICKIES

It's simple to be wise. Just think of something stupid to say, then say the opposite!

Sam Levenson

I once wanted to be an atheist, but I gave it up because they have no holidays!

Henny Youngman

Sex between a man and a woman can be wonderful, provided you get between the right man and the right woman!

Woody Allen

It's been so long since I had sex, I've forgotten who ties up whom!

Joan Rivers

The most remarkable thing about my mother is that for forty years, she served the family nothing but leftovers. The original meal was never found!

Calvin Trillin

Getting Older

You only live once, but if you work it right, once is enough.

Joe E. Lewis

You know you're getting older when:

You get into your car and the steering wheel is higher than you are;

You're on social security sex—you get a little each month but it's not enough to live on;

You look forward to a dull evening;

A beautiful woman asks you what your sign is and you tell her "Blue Cross";

Happy hour is a nap;

You're walking down the street and someone stops you and says, "Hey, Buddy those are great alligator shoes you're wearing!" And you're not wearing any shoes;

You sink your teeth into a juicy steak and the teeth stay there;

You start ordering a martini with a prune instead of an olive;

The bird singing outside your window is a vulture;

You can't tell the difference between a heart attack and an orgasm;

Filling the bird feeder is a good morning's work;

Bingo has become a spectator sport;

You can tell the same jokes over and over, because no one remembers;

No one cares if you eat melba toast and Jello for dinner;

Your secrets are safe because your friends don't remember them either;

When your wife says she's late, it means she's constipated.

A friend asked me, "Do you believe in the hereafter?"

I said, "Yes, no matter where I am, in the kitchen, in the bedroom, or in the basement, I ask myself, "What am I here after?"

I don't want to say I'm old...but when I was young, the Dead Sea was only sick.

I don't harass women, I just love to rub up against them.

A new Jewish porno film just came out. Its called, "Debbie Does Dishes."

"I'm making another Jewish porno film! ten percent sex and ninety percent guilt!"

If you talk dirty to women, you get one year in jail. If they talk dirty to you, it cost five dollars a minute.

A doctor says to a man after an exam, "You're pregnant!"

The man says, "How does a man become pregnant?"

The doctor says, "The usual way. ...A little wine, a little dinner...."

Henny Youngman

I told my wife I may have winter in my hair, but I have summer in my heart. She said, "I'd rather see a little spring in your ass."

A skeleton walked into a bar. He said, "Give me a beer and a mop."

The phone rings and a woman says, "Helloooo."

A man's voice says, "I know what you want. You want me to massage your legs and run my hands over your whole body. You want me to put my tongue in your ear!"

She says, "All that you get from one hello!"

Getting Older

more one-liners

My memory is not as sharp as it used to be. Also my memory is not as sharp as it used to be.

———

Do you know how to prevent sagging? Just eat 'til the wrinkles fill out.

———

I've still got it, but nobody wants to see it.

———

People our age can still enjoy an active, passionate sex life. Provided we get cable or that dish thing.

———

These days, about half the stuff in my shopping cart says, "For fast relief." It's scary when you start making the same noises as your coffeemaker.

———

Any woman can have the body of a 21-year-old...as long as she buys him a few drinks first.

———

There's a new pill out to stop gambling. If it doesn't work, they promise to give you *double* your money back.

———

My wife is not a great cook. I mean, the meatloaf should not glow in the dark!

She likes wild sex! The other night she tied my hands and feet to the bedposts. Then she got dressed and went out.

I was coming home from a business trip and I asked the cab driver, "Where does a guy go in this town for a good time?" So he took me to my house.

A ninety-four-year-old woman will appear in an upcoming issue of Playboy Magazine. Her photo will be on page 34 and her breasts will be on page 35.

My wife is a sex object. Every time I ask for sex, she objects.

I don't want to achieve immortality through my work. I want to achieve immortality through not dying.

The difference between a northern fairy tale and a southern fairy tale is, a northern fairy tale begins, "Once upon a time," and a southern fairy tale begins, "Y'all ain't gonna believe this shit."

Remember: You don't stop laughing because you grow old. You grow old because you stop laughing!

My Favorite Henny Youngman One-liners

The doctor said, "Stick your tongue out the window."

I said, "What for?"

He said, "I'm mad at my neighbors."

My arm was hurting. The doctor looked at it. Then he said to me, "Have you ever had this pain before?"

I said, "Yes."

He said, "Well, you got it again."

I have a fine doctor. If you can't afford the operation, he touches up the X-rays.

I said to him, "I also have a sore foot."

He said, "I'll have you walking in an hour."

He did. He stole my car!

A lot of people are desperate today. A guy walked up to me and said, "You see any cops around here?"

I said, "No."

He said, "Stick em up!"

The plane was going up and down. A little old lady got very scared. She shouted, "Everybody pray."

One man said, "I don't know how to pray."

She said, "Well, do something religious." So he took up a collection!

———

You know what's embarrassing? When you look through a keyhole and you see another eye.

———

I was in the lobby of a hotel. I looked down and there was a guy's hand in my pocket. I said, "What are you doing?"

He said, "I need a match."

I said, "Why don't you ask for it."

He said, "I don't talk to strangers!"

———

On Valentine's Day, my wife gave me the usual gift. She ate my heart out!

———

I said to my mother-in-law, "My house is your house." Last week she sold it.

———

My wife went to the beauty parlor and got a mud pack. For two days she looked great. Then the mud fell off.

———

This morning, she ran after the garbage truck, yelling, "Am I too late for the garbage?" The garbage man yelled back, "No, jump in."

———

Some people play a horse to win, place, or show. I should have bet my horse to live.

———

The jockey kept hitting his horse. The horse turned around and said, "What are you hitting me for? There's nobody behind us."

One year, a friend went into the breeding business. He tried to cross a rooster with a rooster. You know what he got? A very upset rooster.

One time he crossed a Great Dane with a poodle. No one knows what it is, but when it barks everyone listens.

I came from a very poor family. They couldn't afford to have children, so our neighbors had me.

My wife is so bowlegged, when she sits around the house she really sits around the house!

The cutest little girl was giving me a manicure. I said, "How about some dinner later?"

She said, "I'm married."

I said, "Call your husband and tell him you're going to visit a friend."

She said, "Tell him yourself. He's shaving you."

When I was a kid, I had the cutest little button nose but they couldn't feed me. It was buttoned to my lower lip.

I just solved the parking problem. I bought a parked car.

———

I walked into a store and said, "Today is my wife's birthday. I'd like to buy her a nice pen."

The clerk winked at me and said, "A little surprise, huh?"

I said, "Yeah, she's expecting a Cadillac."

———

I came home the other night and I was stunned. Our car was in the living room. I said to my wife, "How did the car get in the living room?"

She said, "It was easy. I made a left turn at the kitchen."

———

She went down a one-way street and was stopped by a cop. He said to her, "Didn't you see the arrows?"

She said, "I didn't even see the Indians."

———

Well, enough of Henny Youngman (king of the one-liners). I met him once and he was very gracious and friendly.

One-Liners In The News

Southwest Airlines is now charging passengers for an extra seat if they are overweight! The only problem is, the seats are not together!

———

Walgreen's pharmacy is coming out with a new gift package for men. It contains Xenophen, Rogaine and Viagra! I can't think of a better way to tell your special guy that he's fat, bald and impotent!

———

Researchers discovered that it takes one million sperm to fertilize one egg. The reason is: no one stops to ask directions!

———

Pollsters just released a new poll. Eighty percent of Americans are rude to other Americans. When the pollster asked the other twenty percent how they really felt, they told the polster to take his clipboard and shove it where the sun don't shine!

———

The President Clinton Library is open. It is the only presidential library with an adult book section!

———

Clinton has been offered a TV talk show. His show will be different than other talk shows. His guests will be under the desk!

———

Clinton is also looking good. He lost over forty pounds. He can finally get into his own pants!

———

Medical researchers have discovered a new disease that has no symptoms. It's impossible to detect and there is no known cure. Fortunately, no cases have been reported so far!

A doctor reported that a sixty-five-year-old woman gave birth to a baby recently in India. The baby looks just like his eighty-five-year-old father. Bald, no teeth, and wears a diaper!

Men notice and remember a woman's eyes more than seventy percent of any other part of a woman's body. If that's the case, how come there isn't a restaurant chain called "Pupils" instead of "Hooters"?

Discovery Channel noted that the male hyena gets very upset during sex. Who wouldn't with the female laughing at you all the time?!

Short Jokes

Ice Cream Break

A little old man sloooooowly shuffles into an ice cream parlor. He pulls himself slooooowly, painfully, up onto a stool. After catching his breath, he orders a banana split.

The waitress asks kindly, "Crushed nuts?"

"No," he replies, "Arthritis."

Let's Move

Abrams frantically dashed up the stairs of his apartment building. He burst into his apartment yelling to his wife, "Sarah, we got to move out of here right away. I just heard the janitor from this building screwed every woman in it but one."

Sarah said, "Yeah, I know. She's that stuck-up tenant on the third floor."

Jake

Jake was dying. His wife, Becky, was maintaining a candlelight vigil by his side. She held his fragile hand, tears running down her face. Her praying roused him from slumber. He looked up and his pale lips began to move slightly.

"My darling Becky," he whispered.

"Hush, my love," she said. "Rest. Shhhh, don't talk."

He was insistent. "Becky," he said in his tired voice, "I have something I must confess to you."

"There's nothing to confess, everything is okay. Go to sleep."

Jake said, "No, I must die in peace. I slept with your sister, your best friend, and your mother!"

"I know," Becky said. "That's why I poisoned you."

Smith climbs to the top of Mt. Sinai to get close enough to talk to his Maker. Looking up, he asks the Lord, "God, what does a million years mean to you?"

The Lord replies, "A minute."

Smith asks, "And what does a million dollars mean to you?"

The Lord replies, "A penny."

Smith asks, "Can I have a penny?"

The Lord replies, "In a minute."

A man goes to a shrink and says, "Doctor, my wife is unfaithful to me. Every evening, she goes to Larry's bar and picks up men. In fact, she sleeps with anybody who asks her. I'm going crazy. What do you think I should do?"

"Relax," says the doctor. "Take a deep breath and calm down. Now, tell me, exactly where is Larry's bar?"

An old man goes to a wizard to ask him if he can remove a curse he has been living with for the last forty years. The wizard says, "Maybe I can help you, but you will have to tell me the exact words that were used to put the curse on you."

The old man says without hesitation, "I now pronounce you man and wife."

John was on his deathbed and gasped pitifully. "Give me one last request!"

"Of course, John," his wife said softly.

"Six months after I die," he said, "I want you to marry Bob."

"I thought you hated Bob," she said.

With his last breath, John said, "I do!"

A man picks up a young woman in a bar and persuades her to come back to his hotel. When they are relaxing afterwards, he asks, "Am I the first man you ever made love to?"

She looks at him thoughtfully for a second before replying. "You might be," she says. "Your face looks familiar."

Final Exam

A college teacher reminds her class of the next day's final exam. She says, "I won't tolerate any excuses for your not being here tomorrow. I might consider a serious personal injury, illness, or death in the family, but that's it. No other excuses are acceptable!"

A smartass in the back of the room raises his arm and asks, "What would you say if tomorrow I said I was suffering from complete and utter sexual exhaustion?"

The entire class does their best to stifle their snickering. When silence is restored, the teacher smiles at the student and sweetly says, "Well, I guess you'd have to write the exam with your other hand."

Three guys are sitting at a bar when the first guy says, "My wife is so dumb, she carries an automatic garage door opener in her car and she doesn't have an automatic garage door."

The second guy says, "My wife is so dumb, she has a cellular phone antenna on her car and she doesn't even have a cellular phone."

The third guy says, "My wife is so dumb, she carries a purse full of rubbers and she doesn't even have a dick."

A flight attendant was stationed at the departure gate to check tickets. As a man approached, she extended her hand for the ticket and he opened his trench coat and flashed her. Without missing a beat, she said, "Sir, I need to see your ticket, not your stub."

Quickies!

These are very short stories and jokes. I like this kind of humor because it's very fast and usually gets big laughs.

This guy walks into a doctor's office with a big bullfrog sitting on his head. The doctor is a little stunned and says, "Can I help you?"

The frog says, "Yeah, I'd like this wart removed from my ass!"

A forty-year-old man got his member caught in a vacuum cleaner hose. The paramedics answered the call. The man told them his relationship with the vacuum cleaner was purely physical. He didn't want any attachments!

A woman walks into a hardware store to buy some shutters for her windows. While she's looking around, she spots a beautiful teapot and asks the clerk for the price. He says, "It's $100."

She says, "Oh, that's much too expensive, I'll just take the two sets of shutters."

He says to her, "Do ya wanna screw for the hinges?"

She says, "No, but I'll do it for the teapot!"

This guy is outside flying a kite and he can't seem to get it off the ground. His wife has been watching him for a while and finally says to him, "You need a piece of tail!"

He says, "Make up your mind! Yesterday you told me to fly a kite!"

Chapter 13

MY VERY FAVORITE JOKES AND STORIES

Everyone should be able to relate a funny story and get laughs. I will highlight and emphasize where you need to show more emotion and voice modulation. Some people tell jokes and they're funny. Others tell the same jokes and they bomb. Timing and delivery are most important.

For example, someone once said to me, "Buddy! You have great delivery. It should be on the back of a TRUCK!" (Build to the last word, when you say, *truck*...it should be crisp and a bit louder.)

The following jokes and stories are not necessarily in order as to how funny they are:

Natasha

It's 10 p.m. in New York City. It's a dreary, foggy cold night. A man wearing a long fur coat with a matching fur hat and a beard approaches a building on the lower east side of the city. He walks up the seven steps to the front door of a brownstone and knocks rapidly.

A light goes on and the front door opens. Standing there is a woman. She is the madam of this brothel. She carefully looks over this guy with the fur coat and long beard and says," Yes, can I help you?"

He says (with a Russian dialect), "I vant to see Natasha."

The madam says, "Natasha?"

The man repeats himself, "Yes, I vant to see Natasha!"

The madam says, "Natasha gets one thousand dollars a visit."

He says, "No problem!" He whips out one thousand dollars and gives it to the madam. He is shown upstairs to Natasha's room.

The second night, he comes back, knocks on the door, the Madam opens it, sees the same guy and says, "What do you want?"

He again says, "I vant to see Natasha."

The madam says, "Listen, there are no bargains, it's still gonna cost you one thousand dollars to see Natasha."

He whips out the money and goes up to see Natasha. This goes on for three nights. Finally, Natasha says to him, "I've never had a man come to visit me three nights in a row and give me a thousand dollars each time. Where are you from?"

He says, "Minsk!"

She shouts, "Minsk! I have a sister in Minsk!"

He says, "I know. She gave me three thousand dollars to give to you."

The Best Reason

This guy is sitting at a fancy bar when a beautiful woman sits down next to him. She glances at him and he looks back at her with a big smile. She says, "How would you like to have a good time?"

He replies, "I really would, but there are three reasons I can't."

She says, "What are the three reasons?"

He says, "The first reason is, I don't have any money with me."

She says, "Take the other two reasons and shove em up your ass!"

It's Nice To Be Remembered

There's a funeral for this "lady of the evening" and there's quite a turnout at the funeral parlor. The pastor starts his sermon and after the traditional words of prayer he says, "Is there anyone in the audience who would like to say something about our dear, departed friend?"

No one speaks up. The pastor says, "Surely there must be someone who wants to say a few words of remembrance?"

Finally, a little old guy sitting all the way in the back stands up and says, "She gave the best blow job in Las Vegas!"

The audience is stunned. One of the lady of the evening's friends, who also is a hooker, turns to another friend and says, "See, you have to die before they say something good about you!"

Another Hooker Story

This Russian went to a brothel. When he got into the room with the girl, she raised her hands to take off her blouse. The Russian looked and saw she had no hair under her arms. He said, "Vere's da vool? Vot happened to da vool?"

She told him in America, women shave under their arms.

Then she takes off her skirt. The Russian looks at her legs, sees no hair on her legs and says, "Vere's da vool? Vot happened to da vool?"

She again told him that in America, most women shave their legs.

Then, she takes off her panties. The Russian looks at her and says, "Vere's da vool? Vot happened to da vool?"

The girl says to him, "Look, mister, did you come here to knit or to fuck?"

The Urologist: a True Story

A few years ago when I was living in Los Angeles, I was a member of a men's group called the Valley Jesters. The group had about sixty members and met once a month. The Valley Jesters were dedicated to raising money to give to various charities. The members raised money from golf tournaments and charity balls, then donated it.

Each month before the meeting started, members were obliged to get up and relate jokes or funny stories that would make the Jesters laugh. A guest speaker was also invited to the meetings.

One particular evening, a very famous urologist was the guest speaker. He talked about all the parts of a man's reproductive system.

Just before his closing, he made this statement. "There is no better feeling in the world than to have an orgasm!"

One of the older members, about eighty-five years old, stood up and asked the urologist, "Did you ever have a "hole in one?"

Everyone totally cracked up and they laughed for ten minutes! Finally, the urologist said, "That's the best comment I have ever heard."

The Gentleman

A gentleman staying at the Ritz in London removes a card from a telephone book in Picadilly. He gets back to the hotel and calls the number. A lady with a soft voice answers and asks if she can be of assistance.

The gentleman says, "Hello, this is Mr. Thorndike at the Ritz in Room 1409. I'd like a sexual adventure! First, I would like some missionary positions, some Kama Sutra techniques and some mild bondage. I would like to finish up with a sensual massage! What do you think?"

The lady on the phone says, "I think it sounds intriguing, sir, but you might like to press nine to get an outside line!"

Masquerade

This guy goes into a fun shop to get a costume for a masquerade party. He says to the clerk, "What have you got that's really different?"

The clerk says, "I have a great outfit for you. ...I can give you a three-cornered hat, a red vest, black leggings and a flintlock rifle."

The guy says, "How much?"

The clerk says, "That outfit will cost you $85."

The guy says, "Oh, that's too much!"

The clerk says, "Well, how about a two-cornered hat, no vest, the leggings and a pistol."

The guy says, "That sounds great, how much?"

The clerk says, "That outfit will cost you $50."

The guy says, "That's still a little pricey."

The clerk says, "How much do you want to spend?"

The guy says, "I'm thinking in the area of $15 to $20."

The clerk is annoyed and says, "Listen, I have a great idea for you."

The guy asks, "What is it?"

The clerk says, "Take off all your clothes and pour a can of red paint all over your body. Then, take a broomstick and shove it up your ass!"

The guy asks, "Why should I do that?"

The clerk replies, "It's inexpensive and you can go as a jelly apple!"

Union Rules

A dedicated Teamsters union worker was attending a convention in Las Vegas and decided to check out the local brothels.

When he got to the first one, he asked the madam, "Is this a union house?"

"No," she replied, "I'm sorry, it isn't."

"Well, if I pay you $100, what cut do the girls get?"

"The house gets $80 and the girls get $20," she answered.

Mightily offended at such unfair dealings, the union man stomped off down the street in search of a more equitable, hopefully unionized shop.

His search continued until finally he reached a brothel where the madam responded, "Why, yes sir, this is a union house. We observe all union rules."

The man asked, "And if I pay you $100, what cut do the girls get?"

"The girls get $80 and the house gets $20," the madam said.

"That's more like it!" the union man said. He handed the madam $100, looked around the room and pointed to a stunningly attractive blonde.

"I'd like her," he said.

"I'm sure you would, sir," said the Madam. Then she gestured to a ninety-two-year-old woman in the corner, "But Ethel here has 67 years seniority and she's next."

The Prize

A woman meets a gorgeous man in a bar. They talk, they connect, and they end up leaving together. They get back to his place, and as he shows her around his apartment, she notices that his bedroom is packed with sweet cuddly teddy bears.

Hundreds of cute small bears are on a shelf all the way along the floor, cuddly medium-sized ones on a shelf a little higher, and huge enormous bears on the top shelf along the wall.

The woman is surprised that this guy would have a collection of teddy bears, especially one that's so extensive, but she decides not to mention this to him, and actually is quite impressed by his sensitive side.

She turns to him, they kiss, and then they rip each other's clothes off and make hot steamy love. After an intense night of passion with this sensitive guy, they are lying there together in the afterglow, the woman rolls over and asks, smiling, "Well, how was it?"

The guy says: "Help yourself to any prize from the bottom shelf."

Excitement

Then there were these two guys who had gone to the same college and become great friends. During college, they had a great time. Anything that was going on, they were always right in the middle of it.

When they graduated, however, they each went their own separate way. Two or three years later, they ran into one another on the street. They were very happy to see each other, and during the conversation, one of them asked the other what he was doing for work.

"I'm an undertaker," responded the friend.

"That doesn't sound like you. During college, you were always the one looking for excitement."

"There is plenty of excitement in this racket," explained the friend. "Just the other day, I got a call to pick up this stiff in a hotel room. When I entered the room, he was lying there on the bed, stark naked, with a huge erection. I didn't want to take him out like that, so I took a hanger from the closet, and gave it a good swat.

"You want to talk about excitement? I WAS IN THE WRONG ROOM!"

Because I'm a Blonde?

A girl comes skipping home from school and shouts, "Mommy, Mommy! Today we did counting and all the other kids got up to five, but I got up to ten. 1, 2, 3, 4, 5, 6, 7, 8, 9, 10! That's good, isn't it, Mommy?"

"Yes, dear, it is."

"Is that because I'm blonde, Mommy?"

"Yes, dear, it is."

The next day the girl comes skipping home and screams, "Mommy, Mommy! Today we did the alphabet and all the other kids only got to D, but I got up to G. A, B, C, D, E, F, G! Isn't that good, Mommy?"

"Yes, dear, it is."

"Is that because I'm blonde, Mommy?"

"Yes, dear, it is."

The following day the girl comes skipping home and exclaims, "Mommy, Mommy! Today we did gym class, and all the other girls had a flat chest, but I have these!"

At this point the girl pulls up her top, revealing a pair of amazing 36C breasts. "That's good, isn't it, Mommy?"

"Yes, dear, it is," replied the slightly embarrassed mother.

"Is it because I'm blonde, Mommy?"

"No, dear, it's because you're twenty-five."

Ice Fishing

This blonde really wanted to go ice fishing. She'd seen many books on the subject, and finally, after getting all the necessary tools together, she made for the nearest frozen lake.

After positioning her comfy footstool, she started to make a circular cut in the ice. Suddenly—from the sky—a voice boomed, "THERE ARE NO FISH UNDER THE ICE!"

Startled, the blonde moved further down the ice, poured a thermos of cappuccino, and began to cut another hole. Again, from the heavens, the voice bellowed, "THERE ARE NO FISH UNDER THE ICE!"

The blonde, now quite worried, moved way down to the opposite end of the ice, set up her stool, and tried again to cut her hole. The voice came once more, even louder: "THERE ARE NO FISH UNDER THE ICE!"

She stopped, looked skyward, and said, "Is that you, Lord?"

The voice replied, "NO, THIS IS THE ICE RINK MANAGER!"

Cute Blonde

I pulled into a crowded parking lot and rolled down the car windows to make sure my Labrador Retriever had fresh air. She was stretched out on the back seat, and I wanted to impress upon her that she must remain there. I walked to the curb backward, pointing my finger at the car and saying emphatically, "Now you stay. Do you hear me? Stay! Stay!"

The blonde driver of a nearby car rolled down her window and said, "Why don't you just put it in park?"

The Circus Performer

This guy works at the circus but he has a terrible odor. The circus master really likes him and one day calls him into his office. He says, "Barton, everyone here at the circus likes you but you smell real awful!"

Barton says, "I take showers every day and use all kinds of lotions to get rid of the smell!"

The circus master says, "You must go to a doctor to get to the bottom of this!"

Barton goes to the doctor who can't find anything wrong with him.

The doctor asks him, "What kind of work do you do at the circus?"

Barton says, "I work with the elephants, I clean the stalls and sweep up the areas where they live!"

The doc said, "Is that all you do?"

Barton replies, "I also help them when they get constipated. What I have to do is take my fist and ram it up their ass until they relieve themselves!"

The doctor says, "Now I know why you have that odor all the time!"

Barton questions, "What should I do?"

The doctor says, "You should quit your job!"

Barton says, "What—and give up show business!"

Another Circus Story

This giant strong man at the circus weighs over 300 pounds. He was just married to the three-foot-tall girl midget. The giant's friend wanted to ask him a very personal question and said, “Cosmo, how does a guy your size have sex with such a small girl?”

Cosmo says, “Well, I pick her up and move her back and forth on my pecker.”

His friend says, “But isn’t that like jacking off?”

Cosmo says, “Yeah, but at least you have someone to talk to!”

The Movies

This guy goes out and buys a chicken for dinner. He likes everything fresh, so he buys a live chicken and plans to kill it at home and take the feathers off himself.

On the way home, he decides to go to the movies to see a film he had missed. Since the theater doesn’t allow live creatures inside, he puts the chicken in his pants to hide it.

When he sits down, the chicken starts to move around, so he opens his fly so that the chicken can get some air. The chicken gets nervous, so it sticks his head out of the fly.

Two women sit down next to the man and the movie starts.

One woman says to the other woman, “I think the guy sitting next to me has his penis out.”

The other woman says, “Don’t pay any attention to him.”

The first woman says, “I’m not paying attention to him, but the damn thing is eating my popcorn!”

Two Weeks Later...

These same two woman are sitting at the movies two weeks later. One of the women says, "Mabel, there's a guy sitting next to me, playing with himself."

Mabel says, "Let's move to the next row."

Her friend says, "I can't."

Mabel says, "Why not?"

Her friend says, "Because he's using my hand!"

The Ventriloquist

This ventriloquist can't get any work. He constantly calls his agent looking for work. His agent tells him, "They are not booking ventriloquists. There are absolutely no calls for your type of entertainment."

The ventriloquist says, "I need to work, get me anything!"

The agent thinks for a minute, then says, "You know, I just got a call from a fortune teller. She's looking for a medium."

The ventriloquist says, "What's a medium?"

The agent says, "You know, someone who communicates with the dead."

The ventriloquist says, "I can't do that."

The agent says, "Sure you can! With your talent, you can throw your voice and make it seem you're talking to their dear departed relatives."

Well, he needs the work, so he goes to see the fortune teller. She gives him a big turban with a fancy purple robe with a half crescent in gold embroidered on it and tells him to do his stuff.

The first client that comes into the parlor is an older woman. He says, "May I help you, Madam?"

She says, "Do you communicate with the dear departed?"

He says, "Yes, I do!"

She says, "How much will it cost to speak to my dear departed husband?"

He says, "For your husband to talk to you, would cost $50. For you to talk to your husband and get a response from him would cost you $75."

The ventriloquist then says to her, "However, for your husband to talk to you while I'm drinking a glass of water will cost you $100."

The Theater

A man was sprawled across three entire seats in a theater. When the usher came by and noticed this, he whispered to the man, "Sorry, sir, but you're only allowed one seat."

The man groaned, but didn't budge.

The usher became impatient. "Sir," the usher said, "if you don't get up from there, I'm going to have to call the manager."

Again the man just groaned, which infuriated the usher, who turned and marched briskly back up the aisle in search of the manager. In a few moments, both the usher and the manager returned and stood over the man.

Together, the two of them repeatedly tried to move the man, but to no avail. Finally, they called the police. The cop arrived and surveyed the situation briefly.

"All right, buddy, what's your name?"

"Sam," the man moaned.

"Where ya from, Sam?" the cop asked.

"The balcony."

The Magician

A magician in Las Vegas is in the last few minutes of his act. He says to the audience, "I need a volunteer. I need a male at least six feet tall and weighing at least 225 pounds."

This kid comes bounding on the stage wearing shorts and a T-shirt and is at least six-feet, five-inches tall, weighing 250 pounds.

The magician asks, "What's your name?"

The guy says, "Joe."

The magician says, "Joe, do you see this aluminum bat I'm holding? I want you on the count of three to hit me as hard as you can right on my head."

Joe says, "Hold it! If I hit you with this bat, I could kill you."

The magician says, "Don't worry, I'm a magician and this is magic. You can hit me as hard as you can."

So Joe picks up the bat and swings the bat as hard as he can. He hits the magician square on the top of his head. The magician goes down and is out cold. They can't revive him and he slips into a coma!

Three months pass and he hasn't moved a muscle. One day, while the nurse is opening up the blinds, she notices the magician opening one eye. The nurse gets very excited and calls the doctor.

He comes rushing in, examines the magician and says to the nurse, "Call his family and friends, I think he's about to come out of the coma."

Everyone is called! They come rushing to the hospital. The room is packed—everyone staring at the magician.

His left eye slowly starts to flutter! His right eye starts to flutter! His nose starts to move from left to right. Slowly his eyes open. He looks around the room and a big smile crosses his face. He raises his arms outward and yells, "TA DAAAH!"

The Little Worker

A young family moved into a house next door to a vacant lot. One day a construction crew turned up to start building a house on the empty lot next door. The young family's five-year-old daughter naturally took an interest in all the activity going on next door and spent much of each day observing the workers.

Eventually the construction crew, all of them gems in the rough, more or less adopted her as a kind of project mascot. They chatted with her, let her sit with them while they had coffee and lunch breaks, and gave her little jobs to do here and there to make her feel important.

At the end of the first week they even presented her with a pay envelope containing a couple of dollars. The little girl took this home to her mother, who said all the appropriate words of admiration and suggested that they take the two dollar "pay" she had received to the bank the next day to start a savings account.

When they got to the bank the teller was equally impressed and asked the little girl how she had come by her very own paycheck at such a young age?

The little girl proudly replied, "I worked last week with the crew building the house next door to us."

"My goodness gracious," said the teller, "and will you be working on the house again this week, too?"

The little girl replied, "I will if those assholes at Home Depot ever deliver the fucking sheet rock..."

Financial Help

One day, I needed a new secretary, but she had to have financial experience to help me with my accounting problems. I interviewed a few prospects and to one woman, whom I later employed, I gave a monetary problem to solve. I said, "If I gave you twenty thousand dollars less sixteen percent, what would you take off?"

She said, "Everything but my earrings."

What's in a Name?

In pharmacology, all drugs have two names, a brand name and a generic name.

For example, the brand name, Tylenol, has a generic name, acetaminophen. Aleve is called "naproxen." Amoxil is called "amoxicillin." Advil is called "ibuprofen."

The FDA has been looking for a generic name for Viagra. After careful consideration by a team of government experts, they recently announced that they have settled on the generic name of "mycoxafloppin." Also considered were "mycoxafailin," "myydixadrupin," "mydixarisin," "mydixadud," "dixafix," and of course, "ibepokin."

AWOL

This soldier doesn't want to go to Iraq. So he runs away and the MPs are in hot pursuit. He sees a nun walking and pleads with her to help him. She looks at him and says, "Quick, get under my skirt."

No sooner does he do this than the MPs are on the scene.

They say, "Sister, have you seen a deserter go by here?'

The sister says, "No." So the MPs leave.

A few minutes later, the soldier comes out from under her skirt and says, "Sister, you saved my life and by the way you have a beautiful pair of legs."

She says, "Go a little higher and you'll find a beautiful pair of balls. I don't want to go to Iraq either!"

A War Story

Forty years after the end of World War II, a Japanese soldier by the name of Taka Mitsia was found holed up in a cave on the island of Guam. He never knew the war ended. He was brought back to Japan as a national hero. When he arrived in Tokyo, thousands of people welcomed him.

After the celebrations ended, he wanted to go back to his little village and be reunited with his wife. When he arrived at the village, he was stopped by an old friend.

His friend said, "Welcome back. You are a great hero but I have some bad news for you."

Taka said, "What is it?"

His friend said, "While you were away, your wife took up with a black man first and then she took up with a Jew."

Taka is shocked. He trudges up the hill to his house, where his wife Fujiama is waiting.

She screams, "Taka, I am so happy that you returned to me after so many years."

Taka walks up to her, hits her in the head and says, "I have been living in a cave for forty years and now when I return, I am told that you took up with a black man and then with a Jew!"

She looks at him and says, "What motherfucker told you those bubba meinzers?"

Planning WW III

President Bush and Colin Powell are sitting in a bar.

A guy walks in and asks the barman, "Isn't that Bush and Powell sitting over there?"

The barman says, "Yep, that's them."

So the guy walks over and says, "Wow, this is a real honor. What are you guys doing in here?"

Bush says, "We're planning WW III."

And the guy says, "Really? What's going to happen?"

Bush says, "Well, we're going to kill forty million Iraqis this time and one blonde with big boobs."

The guy exclaims, "A blonde with big boobs? Why kill a blonde with big boobs?"

Bush turns to Powell and says, "See, I told you no one would worry about the 40 million Iraqis!"

A Postcard

A wealthy man was having an affair with an Italian woman for several years. One night, during one of their rendezvous, she confided in him that she was pregnant. Not wanting to ruin his reputation or his marriage, he paid her a large sum of money if she would move to Italy and secretly have the child.

If she would raise the child, he would also provide child support until the child turned eighteen. She agreed, but asked how he would know when the baby was born.

To keep it discreet, he told her to simply mail him a post card, and write "spaghetti" on the back. He would then arrange for child support payments to begin.

One day, about nine months later, he came home to his confused wife. "Honey," she said, "you received a very strange postcard today."

"Oh, just give it to me and I'll explain it later," he said.

The wife obeyed, and watched as her husband read the card, turned white, and fainted.

On the card was written: "spaghetti, spaghetti, spaghetti. ...Two with meatballs, one without."

Who's Louder

These three guys are talkin'—an Italian, a Frenchman and a Jew. They're bragging about their sexual prowess.

The Italian says, "When I make love to my wife, I get her so crazy that she starts screaming like the house is on fire."

The Frenchman, not to be outdone, says, "When I make love to my wife we have to board up all the windows. Otherwise the neighbors think I'm killing her, that's how loud she screams."

The Jewish guy says, "You call that screaming? You guys don't know what screaming is. When we get finished making love, all I gotta do is wipe my pecker on the drapes. You'll hear screaming like you never heard before."

Best Short Joke of the Year

A small boy was lost at a large shopping mall. He approached a uniformed police officer and said, "I've lost my Grandpa!"

The cop asked, "What's he like?"

The little boy replied, "A shot of bourbon and women with big boobs."

The Nudist Colony

A man joins a very exclusive nudist colony. On his first day there he takes off his clothes and starts to wander around. A gorgeous blonde walks by and the man immediately gets an erection.

The woman notices his erection, comes over to him and says, "Did you call for me?"

The man says, "No."

She says, "Let me explain! It's a rule here that if you get an erection it implies that you called for me."

She leads him to the side of the pool, lies down on a towel, eagerly pulls him to her and happily lets him have his way with her.

The man continues to explore the facilities. He enters the sauna and as he sits down, he farts. Within minutes, a large hairy man lumbers out of the steam room toward him.

"Did you call for me?" says the hairy man. "You see, if you fart here, that implies that you called for me." The huge man spins him around, bends him over and has his way with him.

The newcomer staggers back to the colony's office, where he is greeted by the naked receptionist.

The man yells, "Here's my membership card. You can keep the $500 membership fee!"

"But sir," she replies, "You've only been here a few hours and haven't had a chance to see all our facilities."

"Listen, lady, I'm sixty-eight years old, I only get an erection once a month, but I fart fifteen times a day! I'm outta here."

The Butler

A butler works for this very wealthy woman. The woman says, "Jeremy, please come up to my bedroom at once!" So Jeremy goes upstairs and enters his mistress's bedroom.

The woman says, "Jeremy, come over here!"

"Yes, ma'am!" says Jeremy.

The woman says, "Jeremy, I want you to take off my dress."

Jeremy says, "Yes, ma'am!" He takes off her dress.

The woman says, "Now, Jeremy take off my brassiere."

"Yes, ma'am!" says Jeremy.

The woman says, "Now take off my stockings."

Jeremy again obeys and says, "Yes, ma'am!"

The woman now says, "Jeremy, now I want you to take off my panties."

He says, "Of course, ma'am."

The woman says, "Jeremy, if I ever catch you wearing my clothes again, you're fired!"

The Crystal Ball

Hillary Clinton goes to a fortune teller to find out what her future holds for her. The fortune teller looks into her crystal ball and lets out a sigh.

Hillary says to her, "What do you see?"

The fortune teller says, "There is no easy way to tell you this, so I'll be blunt. Your husband, Bill, will die a violent death very soon!"

Visibly shaken, Hillary stares at the fortune teller's face, then stares at the candle, then down at her hands. She takes a few deep breaths to compose herself and says to the fortune teller, "Can I ask you a question?"

The fortune teller said, "Of course."

Hillary steadies her voice, which is overcome with emotion and says, "Will I be acquitted?"

Tim buk tu!

Two guys are applying for the same job at an advertising agency. The employer says to them, "I'm gonna give you a problem to solve. I want each of you to write copy for a creative project that we are going to do. You can use prose or any method you need to get across the message. However, the message you create must include the word

"Tim buk tu." You have fifteen minutes to complete the project."

The first applicant thought a while, then he wrote the following:

"While I was working on the shore...listening to the ocean's roar…

"A mighty ship came into view. ...Destination Tim buk tu."

He gave it to the boss, who read it and said, "Very good!" and then looked at the second applicant and said, "Now what about you?"

This is what the other guy wrote.

"Tim and I a-walking went. ...We spied three maidens in a tent.

"Since they be three and we be two...

"I bucked one, and Tim bucked two!"

The Pirate

This story takes place in the time when piracy was rampant in the Caribbean. The pirates attacked helpless villages and raped and pillaged. A young seaman came into one of the most violent ports looking for a job on a vessel. He went into the Pirates' Den, a notorious bar in Port-au-Prince, and sat down with a pint of ale.

In walked this huge man with a patch on one eye, a wooden leg, and a hook instead of a hand. He proceeded to sit down right next to the young seaman. He ordered a large ale and said to the seaman, "How are you, lad? My name is Captain Blood. I am the most feared pirate in these parts."

Naturally, the young seaman was a little scared. He kept staring at the pirate, who said to him, "Join me in a drink, lad. Where ye from, and where ye heading?"

The young sailor got up enough courage and asked the pirate if he would answer a few questions. The pirate said, "Aye, laddie, fire away," as he swigged down his ale.

The seaman said, "My first question is, if it's not being too personal, where did you get the wooden leg?"

The pirate replied, "Aye, laddie, that was a mean one. I was on the poop deck in the most fearsome storm. One of the yardarms broke loose and smashed into my leg, tearing it off at the knee!"

The seaman asked, "What about your hand?"

The pirate replied, "Aye, lad, that's a real horror tale. Me and me mates were attacking a Spanish galleon loaded with jewels and fine clothes. During the attack, I was on the forward deck when I found myself surrounded by the enemy. I drew me sword and attacked! Swinging wildly, I took out a lot of the enemy, but one of them got in a lucky strike and took me hand from me body."

The young seaman said, "Can I ask one more question?

The pirate said, "Buy me a drink and you can ask all the questions you want."

The seaman asked, "How did you get that eye patch?"

The pirate replied, "Well, laddie, it was a bright summer day, not a cloud in the sky. I looked up to the heavens and just then a seagull flew over and dropped his load right into me eye."

"You mean the seagull blinded you?"

Captain Blood answered, "Ahh, no lad! When all that crap hit me eye, I went to wipe it out and forgot I had a hook instead of a hand!"

Another Bar Story

Mike, who is not very bright, is having a drink when this gorgeous girl walks in and sits down next to him at the bar. Wasting no time, he glances at her and says, "Can I buy you a drink?"

She replies, "You can buy me a drink, but that isn't going to get you anywhere with me. It happens that I'm a lesbian!"

He asks her, "What's a lesbian?"

She says, "You gotta be kidding."

Mike says, "No, I don't really know."

In exasperation, she says to him, "Let me explain. I like girls, I like to fondle their breasts, kiss them all over their bodies and make passionate love to them."

He replies, "Wow, I guess I'm a lesbian, too!"

Bank of America

A little old lady went into the Bank of America carrying a bag of money. She insisted she must speak to the president of the bank to open a savings account because she had a lot of money.

She was finally escorted into the president's office, who asks her how much she would like to deposit. She says she has $165,000 and then dumps it out of the bag onto his desk.

The president is surprised and curious how she came by all the cash, so he asks her about it. The lady says, "I make bets!"

The president replies, "Bets? What kind of bets?"

She says, "Well, for example, I'll bet you $25,000 that your balls are square."

The president says, "That's a stupid bet, you can never win with that kind of bet."

The old lady says, "So, would you like to take my bet?"

The president says, "Sure, I'll bet you $25,000 that my balls are not square!"

The little old lady says, "Okay, but since there is a lot of money involved, is it okay if I bring my lawyer with me tomorrow at 10 a.m. to be the witness?"

"Sure," says the president. That night, the president got very nervous about the bet and spent a long time in front of the mirror checking his balls, turning them from side to side and thoroughly checking them to be sure that his balls were not square.

The next morning at 10 a.m., the little old lady appears with her lawyer at the president's office. She introduces the lawyer to the president and repeats the bet. They all agree and the old lady asks the president to drop his pants so they can see.

The president does it. The old lady looks at his balls, and then asks if she can feel them. "Well, okay," he says. Then he notices that the lawyer is quietly banging his head against the wall, so he asks the old lady, "What's wrong with the lawyer?"

The old lady says, "Nothing, except I bet him $100,000 that by 10 a.m. today, I'd have the Bank of America's president's balls in my hands."

The Bus Stop

This beautiful woman is standing by a bus stop. She is wearing a black leather jacket, a pair of black leather high boots and a very tight black leather skirt. The bus arrives and the door swings open. She starts to step up to the first step, but her skirt is too tight. So she reaches back behind her and pulls the zipper at the top of her skirt down.

She again tries to step up on the bus. Her skirt is still too tight. She reaches back again and pulls the zipper down a little more. She still can't get up the steps.

The bus driver is getting very frustrated. As she goes to try again to step up, she suddenly feels two hands encircle her waist and she is picked up bodily and placed on the bus. She turns around and sees a big guy with a big grin on his face holding her.

She says, "How dare you put your hands on me? I don't even know you."

He says, "Lady, after you pulled the zipper down on my pants two times, I figured we were good friends!"

A Heavy Drinker

Tom takes his date to a wild party. They are drinking booze in large quantities. Fortunately, Tom's date is not that heavy a drinker. They decide to leave. She helps to get him to his car and she gets behind the wheel. After driving for a little while, he says to her, slurring his words, "Stop the car. I have to take a pee."

She stops the car by the side of the road. She has to get out of the car to help him out because he's so drunk, he can't even open his fly. So she helps him with that and then they get back in the car.

After a few minutes, he says, "I have to pee again!"

She says, "You just went! I even helped you because you're so drunk."

"You really helped me pee?" he says, still slurring his words. "You opened my fly?"

She says, "I did."

He asks, "Then, you took out my pee-pee?"

She says, "Yes, I did."

He then asks her, "Did you shake it off before you put it back in my pants?"

She says, "How am I supposed to know that you're supposed to shake it off before you put it back in your pants!"

He looks at her and says, "You know something, you don't know how to piss!"

Bifocals

This guy gets his first pair of bifocals and is having trouble trying to adjust to them. He's at a party and decides to go to the restroom. He returns a few minutes later and his pants are soaking wet.

His friend says to him, "Your pants are wet, what happened?"

He looks down and says, "Well, I unzipped my fly, and when I took out my pecker, I saw two of them...so I put one back!"

Bite The Bullet

A woman, pregnant with triplets, was walking down the street when a masked robber ran out of the bank and shot her three times in the stomach. She was taken to the hospital.

Luckily, the babies were okay. The surgeon decided to leave the bullets in because it was too risky to operate. She gave birth to two healthy daughters and one healthy son.

All was fine for sixteen years. Then, one day, one of the daughters walks into the room in tears.

"What's wrong?" asks the mother.

The daughter replies, "I was taking a pee and this bullet came out."

The mother tells her it's okay, and explains what happened sixteen years ago.

About a week later, the second daughter walks into the room in tears with the same story. Again, the mother tells her not to worry and explains the story.

A week after that her son walks into the room in tears. "It's okay," says the mom, "I know what happened...you were taking a pee and a bullet came out."

"No," says the boy. "I was playing with myself and I shot the dog."

Five Paces

Barbara Walters did a TV show on gender roles in Kabul several years before the Afghan conflict. She noted that women customarily walked about five paces behind their husbands.

She returned to Kabul recently and observed that women still walk behind their husbands but now seem to walk even further back and are happy with the old custom.

Ms. Walters approached one of the Afghani women and asked, "Why do you now seem happy with the old custom that you used to try to change?"

"Land mines," answered the woman.

Ed Pizza

Ed is in the hospital recovering from an operation. All the nurses are whispering about how small Ed's penis is and how he has his name tattooed on his penis. As he starts to recover, he gets playful with some of the nurses. None of the nurses want to get serious with him and are always snickering about how small his joint is.

But one of the nurses feels sorry for him, goes into his room and gives him an alcohol rub. She comes out of the room later with a big smile on her face.

All the nurses want to know why she's smiling. She tells them, "It's true that Ed seems to have a small penis but when I was giving him an alcohol rub, I happened to accidentally brush by his penis and he got aroused very quickly. I couldn't believe how it grew. Not only was his name tattooed on it but as it got bigger, I noticed that it said, "Ed's Pizza and Catering Service. We deliver at all times...twenty four hours a day, in New Jersey call (201) 443-6758, in Manhattan call (718) 567-2349, in Connecticut call…"

From Outer Space

After traveling for many years, this space ship lands on Earth. Policemen and soldiers surround it as it lands. A large crowd gathers to watch with great expectations for the appearance of space travelers.

Finally, the space ship door opens and a very strange looking creature descends. He raises his arms and with a loud voice says, “Greetings, Earthlings! I have traveled many light-years without touching another planet.”

A spokesman from the crowd asks him, “What are your first requests after traveling so many years to get here?”

The alien looks at him and says, “Take...me...to...your...toilet!”

The Waiter

Two friends went out to a new restaurant for dinner. They noticed that the waiter who took the order carried a spoon in his shirt pocket. It seemed strange to them. When the busboy brought the water and utensils, the friends noticed that he also had a spoon in his pocket.

When the waiter returned to their table, one of the guys asked the waiter, “Why the spoon in your shirt pocket?”

“Well,” he explained, “The restaurant owner hired a consulting firm to revamp all their procedures. After several months of analysis, they concluded that the spoon was the most frequently dropped utensil. They suggested that if the waiters were better prepared, the number of trips to the kitchen would be reduced, thus saving time. One of the guys dropped his spoon and the waiter was able to replace it with his spare spoon.”

The diner also noticed that there was a string hanging out of the waiter's fly. So he asked the waiter, "Excuse me, but can you tell me why you have that string hanging there?"

The waiter said, "Well, the consulting firm that was hired also discovered that we can save time in the restroom. By tying this string to the tip of our member, we can pull it out without touching it and eliminate the need to wash our hands, shortening the time spent in the restroom."

The diner then asked, "After you take it out, how do you put it back?"

The waiter replied in a whispered voice, "I don't know about the others, but I use the spoon!"

Survey

I hate those hoax warnings, but this one is important:

If someone comes to your front door saying they are conducting a survey and asks you to take your clothes off, do not do it! This is a scam; they only want to see you naked. I wish I was warned about this yesterday. I feel so stupid and cheap.

The Check Bounced

This elderly gentleman is walking along Rodeo Drive in Beverly Hills late in the afternoon with this young beautiful woman. They pass a jewelry store with a glittering display of jewelry in its window.

She says to him, "Darling, wouldn't it be nice if you bought me a little gift?"

He says, "That's a very good idea." So they enter the store.

A salesman approaches them and says, "How can I help you?"

The elderly gentleman says, "I'd like to see a diamond ring for this young lady."

She explains, "Oh that's so sweet of you, Bernard."

He says, "Think nothing of it, my darling."

The salesman proceeds to take out some very expensive rings. Bernard says to her, "My dear, why don't you pick out something you like."

She gasps and says, "Darling, are you serious?"

He says, "Of course, my dear."

She picks out a magnificent ring with a three-carat diamond. Then, she says to the salesman, "I like this."

Bernard says to the salesman, "How much is it?"

The salesman says, "That ring is $75,000."

Bernard then says, "That's fine. I'll give you a check for it and will pick up the ring Monday, as soon as the check clears the bank."

The salesman is thrilled and says, "Yes, sir!"

They leave the store very happy and she is hugging and squeezing Bernard. On Monday afternoon, the salesman calls Bernard and says he is very distraught.

"Sir, the bank just called and it seems that there are no funds in your account to cover the cost of the diamond ring. Is there some kind of mistake?"

The old man says, "No, there is no mistake. There is no money in my checking account."

The salesman says, "How could you do this?"

Bernard then says to him, "I know that you are extremely unhappy about this situation, but let's look on the bright side. I had a wonderful weekend."

Rumors—Something to Keep in Mind

Keep this philosophy in mind the next time you either hear, or are about to repeat a rumor:

In ancient Greece (469–399 BC), Socrates was widely lauded for his wisdom. One day the great philosopher came upon an acquaintance who ran up to him excitedly and said, "Socrates, do you know what I just heard about one of your students?"

"Wait a moment," Socrates replied. "Before you tell me, I'd like you to pass a little test. It's called the Triple Filter Test."

"Triple Filter?"

"That's right," Socrates continued. "Before you talk to me about my student, let's take a moment to filter what you're going to say. The first filter is Truth. Have you made absolutely sure that what you are about to tell me is true?"

"No," the man said, "actually I just heard about it and—"

"All right," said Socrates. "So you don't really know if it's true or not. Now let's try the second filter, the filter of Goodness. Is what you are about to tell me about my student something good?"

"No, on the contrary—"

"So," Socrates continued, "you want to tell me something bad about him, even though you're not certain it's true?"

The man shrugged, a little embarrassed.

Socrates continued. “You may still pass the test though, because there is a third filter—the filter of Usefulness. Is what you want to tell me about my student going to be useful to me?”

“No, not really.”

“Well,” concluded Socrates, “if what you want to tell me is neither True, nor Good, nor even Useful, why tell it to me at all?”

The man felt defeated and ashamed. This is the reason Socrates was a great philosopher and held in such high esteem.

It also explains why he never found out that Plato was banging his wife!

Once Upon A Time

Once upon a time, in a land far away, a beautiful, independent, self-assured princess happened upon a frog as she sat on the shores of a pond in a meadow near her castle.

The frog hopped upon the princess’ lap and said, “Beautiful lady, I was once a handsome prince until an evil witch cast a spell on me. One kiss from you, and I will turn back into the handsome young prince that I am, and then we can marry and set up housekeeping in your castle with my mother. You can prepare my meals, clean my clothes, bear my children and feel grateful and happy doing so.”

That night, as the princess dined on a repast of sauteed frog legs in a white wine sauce, she chuckled and thought to herself, “I don’t fucking think so.”

Stranded

Two lawyers are stranded on a deserted island for years. There is nothing for miles around them but water. One of the lawyers tells the other he's going to climb a tree to look for possible ships. The other lawyer says he's crazy and wasting his time.

The lawyer climbs the tree anyway. He gets to the top and says, "This can't be true, I can't believe what I'm seeing!"

The lawyer on the ground yells up, "What do you see?"

So the lawyer on the tree climbs down and tells the other that he saw a naked blonde woman swimming toward their island. The other lawyer starts to laugh, thinking his friend lost his mind.

Within a few minutes, up swims a naked blonde woman, who passes out on the beach. The two lawyers run over to where the woman is lying and one says to the other, "Do you think we should screw her?"

The other lawyer responds, "Out of what!"

By the Numbers

This story takes place in a prison, where it is a known fact that most jokes—dirty and otherwise—are made-up. There are so many jokes told in the prisoners' offtime that instead of going through the whole joke they have a numbering system.

So about eight guys are sitting around telling jokes. One prisoner says, "4-6-7-2," and they all get hysterical. Another guy says, "6-1-7-9," and some of the guys fall down laughing.

A new prisoner sitting among them says to the guy next to him, "Why is everyone getting hysterical when someone gives out four numbers?"

The guy next to him says, "Well, those are really the punch lines of jokes, since we have so many jokes to tell, it goes quicker just to give the numbers."

The guy says, "You're kidding! Can I try it?"

They all say, "Sure!" So he thinks for a minute and he says, "This is a good one: 1-3-9-6."

There's not a sound in the room. He looks around slowly and says, "How come everyone laughed when the other guys gave numbers and no one laughed at my numbers?"

One of the prisoners says to him, "Because your delivery stinks."

Don't Drink and Drive

A policeman pulls over a driver for swerving in and out of lanes on the highway. He tells the guy to blow a breath into a breathalyzer.

"I can't do that, officer."

"Why not?"

"Because I'm an asthmatic. I could get an asthma attack if I blow into that tube."

"Okay, we'll just get a urine sample down at the station."

"Can't do that either, officer."

"Why not?"

"Because I'm a diabetic. I could get low blood sugar if I pee in a cup."

"All right, we could get a blood sample."

"Can't do that either, officer."

"Why not?"

"Because I'm a hemophiliac. If I give blood I could die."

"Fine then, just walk this white line."

"Can't do that either, officer."

"Why not?"

"Because I'm drunk!"

The Open Fire

Christmas was coming up and this guy decided to go out early and get his wife a gift. He remembered her talking about how much she missed having a pet since she had married him, so he thought that he would go buy her a pet.

He drove to the nearest pet store and walked in. He asked the manager what he thought a good pet for his wife would be. The manager showed him around the store, first at the puppies and dogs then at the cats, the fishes, and so on until he finally got to the bird section.

One of the birds caught the man's eye. "Wow, what a beautiful bird," he said.

The manager looked at the man and replied, "This bird is named Chess. He's a talking parrot and he is a perfect holiday gift!"

He took out a lighter and showed the man that if you lit the lighter under Chess' right foot, he would sing "Jingle Bells," and if you lit the lighter under his left foot he would sing "Silent Night."

The man was astonished by this and told the manager that he would take the bird.

Christmas came and the husband and his wife exchanged gifts. After the husband had received the tie and shirt his wife had bought him, he came out with a big object covered by a blanket. He set the object down on the table and uncovered the bird to show his wife.

She loved it! He went on telling her that if you lit a match or lighter under the bird's feet that it sang different holiday songs.

So the wife quickly got a lighter, took the bird out of the cage and lit the lighter under the bird's right foot. The parrot started singing, "Jingle bells, jingle bells, jingle all the way, hey,"

His wife smiled with happiness. She then lit the lighter under Chess' left foot and it started to sing "Silent Night." After the second song the wife said, "I wonder what would happen if you lit the lighter in between Chess's two feet."

"Try it," replied her husband. So she did and all of a sudden the bird opened its mouth and started singing, "Chestnuts roasting on an open fire."

Why Condoms Come in Boxes of 3, 6, and 12

A man walks into a drug store with his 8-year-old son. They happen to walk by the condom display, and the boy asks, "What are these, Dad?"

To which the man matter-of-factly replies, "Those are called condoms, son. Men use them to have safe sex."

"Oh, I see," replied the boy pensively. "Yes, I've heard of that in health class at school." He looks over the display and picks up a package of three and asks, "Why are there three in this package?"

Dad replies, "Those are for high school boys, one for Friday, one for Saturday, and one for Sunday."

"Cool," says the boy. He notices a six-pack and asks, "Then who are these for?"

"Those are for college men," Dad answers, "Two for Friday, two for Saturday, and two for Sunday."

"WOW!" exclaims the boy, "Then who uses THESE?" he asks, picking up a twelve-pack.

With a sigh and a tear in his eye, Dad replies, "Those are for married men. One for January, one for February, one for March."

Jim and Edna

Jim and Edna were both patients in a mental hospital. One day while they were walking past the hospital swimming pool, Jim suddenly jumped into the deep end. He sank to the bottom of the pool and stayed there. Edna promptly jumped in to save him. She swam to the bottom and pulled Jim out.

When the medical director became aware of Edna's heroic act, he immediately ordered her to be discharged from the hospital as he now considered her to be mentally stable.

When he went to tell Edna the news he said, "Edna, I have good news and bad news. The good news is you're being discharged, since you were able to rationally respond to a crisis by jumping in and saving the life of another patient. I have concluded that your act displays soundness of mind. The bad news is that Jim, the patient you saved, hung himself right after you saved him, with his bathrobe belt, in the bathroom."

Edna replied, "He didn't hang himself...I put him there to dry."

Headaches

The doctor said to Joe, "The good news is I can cure your headaches. The bad news is that it will require castration. You have a very rare condition which causes your testicles to press up against the base of your spine and the pressure creates one hell of a headache. The only way to relieve the pressure is to remove the testicles."

Joe was shocked and depressed. He wondered if he had anything to live for. He couldn't concentrate long enough to answer, but decided he had no choice but to go under the knife.

When he left the hospital, he was headache-free for the first time in over twenty years, but he felt as if he were missing an important part of himself.

As he walked down the street he realized he felt like a different person. He could make a new beginning and live a new life. He saw a men's clothing store and thought, "That's what I need, a new suit."

The elderly salesman eyed him quickly and said "Let's see, you're a size forty-four long."

Joe laughed and said, "That's right, how did you know?"

"Been in the business sixty years!"

Joe tried on the suit. It fit perfectly. As Joe admired himself in the mirror, the tailor asked, "How about a new shirt?"

Joe thought for a moment and then said, "Sure."

"Let's see, sixteen-and-a-half neck, thirty-four sleeve."

Joe was surprised. "How did you know?"

"Been in the business sixty years."

The shirt fit perfectly.

As Joe looked at himself in the mirror, the salesman said, "You could use new shoes."

Since Joe was on a roll, he said, "Sure."

The man eyed Joe's feet and said, "nine-and-a-half E."

Joe was astonished. "That's right. How did you know?"

"Been in the business sixty years."

Joe tried on the shoes and they also fit perfectly.

As Joe walked comfortably around the shop, the salesman asked, "How about new underwear?"

Joe thought for a second and said, "Why not."

The man stepped back, eyed Joe's waist and said, "Let's see, size thirty-six."

Joe laughed. "Finally I've got you! I've worn size thirty-two since I was eighteen years old."

The tailor shook his head. "You can't wear a size thirty-two. Size thirty-two underwear would press your testicles against the base of your spine and give you one hell of a headache!"

The Neighbor

Mr. Smith is playing football in his back yard with his son, Johnny. He tells him to run out and he will throw him a pass. The son starts to run near the neighbor's fence dividing the two properties.

His father throws a long pass out of the reach of his son. In fact, the football goes flying over the fence into the neighbor's backyard. His son jumps up to the top of the fence and looks into the neighbor's back yard.

He yells to his dad, "Mr. Jones has the football!"

Then, Johnny says to Mr. Jones, "Can you please throw the football back into our yard?"

Mr. Jones says, "No! It's in my yard and I'm going to keep the football."

Johnny turns and says to his father, "Dad, Mr. Jones won't give us back the football."

Johnny's dad gets very angry. "Whatta you mean he won't give us back the football?"

Johnny says, "That's what he said, Dad!"

His father says, "We'll see about that!"

Johnny's father climbs up and over the fence into Mr. Jones' backyard, confronting him and yelling, "What the hell do mean you won't give me back our football?"

Mr. Jones replies, "Listen, you jerk, first of all the ball is on my property, second of all, you have no right to be in my yard. I could call the police and have you thrown in jail for trespassing. But I'll tell you what I'll do. I've never liked you from the time you moved in next door but I'll give you a chance to get the football back."

The father says, "What do I have to do?"

Jones says, "OK, you want it back, this is how to get it. You hit me as hard as you can! If you put me out, then you win and get the football back."

Johnny's father says, "What happens if I don't put you away?"

Jones says, "Then I hit you and if you don't get up I keep the football. In fact, you can hit me first."

Mr. Smith says, "OK!" Then he winds up and hits Jones as hard as he can in the groin. Mr. Jones doubles up in extreme pain, falls to the ground and for ten minutes can hardly breathe.

When he finally gets up, he says to Johnny's father, "Now, it's my turn."

Johnny's father looks at him and says, "You know something (waving his hand in Jones's face) you can keep the ball!"

You Gotta Be Kiddin' Me

A lot of people asked me where the saying, "you gotta be kiddin' me" came from. It so happens I know. Way back, George Washington was crossing the Delaware River with his troops. They were packed into the boats. It was extremely dark and storming furiously. The water was tossing them back and forth.

Finally, Washington grabbed Corporal Peters and stationed him at the front of the boat with a lantern. He ordered him to keep swinging it so they could see where they were heading. Corporal Peters stood up braving the wind and driving rain, swinging the lantern back and forth.

A while later a big gust of wind hit and threw Corporal Peters and his lantern into the Delaware. Washington and his troops searched for hours trying to find Corporal Peters but to no avail. All of them felt terrible, for the Corporal had been one their favorites.

An hour later Washington and his troops landed on the other side, wet and totally exhausted. He rallied the troops and told them they must go on. After awhile, Washington and his men could go no further. One of his men said, "General, I see lights ahead."

They trudged towards the lights and came upon a huge house there in the woods. What they didn't know was this was a house of ill repute, hidden in the forest to serve all who came.

General Washington pounded on the door, his men crowding around him. The door swung open and the madam looked out to see Washington and all his men. A huge smile came across her face to see so many men standing there.

Washington spoke up. “Hello, ma’am. I’m General George Washington and these are my men. We’re tired and exhausted and desperately need warmth and comfort for awhile.”

Again the madam looked at all the men standing there and with a broad smile on her face said, “Well, General, you have come to the right place. We can surely give you warmth and comfort. How many men do you have?”

Washington replied, “Well, ma’am, there are thirty-two of us without Peters.”

She looked at him and said, “You gotta be kiddin’ me.”

Chapter 14

PHOENIX RISING AND THE SENIOR CLASS

There are many stories about living in Arizona and they are all true! The following lines will give you an idea of what Arizona is like:

All of our out-of-state friends start to visit from October to March….

People in Arizona think a red light is merely a suggestion…!

We think someone driving a car wearing oven mitts is clever….

We may notice that our car is overheating before we drive it…!

People who have black cars or black upholstery in their cars are automatically assumed to be from out of state…!

We always notice the best parking place is in the shade...!

I discovered that in July, most people drive their cars with two fingers….

We can experience third degree burns if we touch any metal part of our cars. We don't get into our cars with leather seats if we are wearing shorts...!

When someone asks how far you live from a location, it's always in terms of minutes, not miles…!

The water from the cold water tap is the same temperature as the hot one! People here buy salsa by the gallon! We know a swamp cooler is not a happy hour drink….

Phoenix Rising!

After the last earthquake, the exodus began, with Californians leaving in droves for Arizona. The I-10 freeway was bumper to bumper with trucks, vans, cars and any other vehicle that was available.

I even saw some horse-drawn wagons with guys riding shotgun. I guess some frantic people were still afraid of an Indian uprising. At night, they formed a circle of the wagons for protection.

Unfortunately, they formed the circle on the freeway and of course it caused a major traffic jam.

We bought a very nice house in Scottsdale, Arizona a few days after the quake, but didn't get to move there until April. We had to sell our place in California. That was not easy, since everyone else in Southern California had the same idea. It was difficult living with my wife and granddaughter during that time, due to the aftershocks.

Every little shock threw them into a panic and there were 16,000 aftershocks the first few months after the earthquake. It was indeed a very stressful time!

We finally sold our house but before we left California, we decided to have an "estate sale" to sell all the stuff that we weren't going to take to Arizona. People called them estate sales if they had more than three bedrooms.

We only had two bedrooms but an estate sale sounded classier than "garage sale." What a mistake that was! We had to price every item that we wanted to sell and people who came in to buy stuff still asked "How much!"

We opened our doors very early in the morning. There was a long line of buyers waiting to get into the house. We were practically giving stuff away. No matter what we marked the items for, the buyers wanted it for less.

I had over a dozen pair of shoes to sell. They were all my size (nine-and-one-half medium) and one guy said to me, "Do you have any size eleven's?"

I replied very casually, "No, but I'll order a pair for you and you can pick them up next week! (a real schmuck!)

It was as if the locusts had descended on us. They were buying everything! After about two hours, I told our youngest son, Jeffrey, he would have to get up and get dressed.

He refused and I said to him, "Why don't you want to get up?" He answered, "Well, if I leave my bed, you'll sell it."

He was right ! As soon as he went to the bathroom, we sold it.

Finally, that fiasco ended and I made a promise to myself that if ever we had to move again, I would donate everything!

We finally moved into our new house. Once we got settled in the new area, I decided to get involved again in entertaining. I sent a letter to all the senior citizen retirement communities and also to all the old age homes in the Phoenix area, offering my services "gratis."

In the letter, I told them I was a singer and comedian. I also mentioned that my wife has a wonderful singing voice and would be included in the show. I would not charge a fee for performing but they had to pay her because she said to me, "At this stage of my life, nothing is free!"

One of the retirement homes called and asked, "How much does gratis cost?" The first week, I got about ten calls asking when we would be available. I decided we would do two shows a week and I began booking show dates.

Show Biz for Seniors

Our first performance was at the Kivel Home for the Aged in Phoenix. It was a very large facility and their clubhouse theater accommodated about 300 people. When we got to the home, the theater was already packed.

We proceeded to set up my karaoke machine and the speakers. The audience watched every move we were making. The setup took about twenty minutes and we were ready to start our show.

Gloria and I went behind the stage curtain waiting for our introduction. We waited and waited, and finally, when I was about to go out on the stage to find out what was taking so long, we heard a small voice start the introduction.

"Can everyone hear me? My name is Shirley Finebaum and I'm your mistress of ceremonies for this evening. I also am celebrating my ninety-fifth birthday today...(applause) so try to be nice to me tonight!"

A light applause followed by some shouting, "Speak louder," and someone else yelled out, "Start the damn show already, I'm getting tired."

Shirley continued, "It's my pleasure to introduce Gloria and Buddy Stein, who will be the entertainers tonight. I think they have appeared on many television shows and other things. They are wonderful human beings, to come here tonight to perform for us gratis!"

An old guy yelled out, "What the hell is gratis?"

Shirley responded, "I'm not sure! but you can ask them yourself after the show."

After this introduction, I finally walked out on the stage. I said, "Hi, everybody! I'm Buddy Stein! Tonight, we're gonna have a lot of fun!"

As I looked into the audience, half the people in the first row were sleeping. I then introduced my wife and they perked up a little. I switched on the karaoke and my wife and I started to sing "On a Wonderful Day Like Today."

The audience loved us! Halfway through our performance we had to stop and give the audience a five minute oxygen break. I told my friends we would have gotten a standing ovation but no one could stand up.

That first year in Phoenix we did about fifty shows for the old age homes. It was a fun time and very gratifying to be able to bring some laughter and songs to these seniors.

Entertaining during our first year in Arizona was my first step to making a comeback into show business. I don't remember ever being anywhere. Ahh! I never stop fantasizing!

The Senior Class

I was already into my third year in Scottsdale. We continued doing shows at retirement homes during the second and third year but not as many as we did the first year.

Gloria wouldn't rehearse because she was busy doing her art work, which is her first passion. She said, "I've had enough of show business."

I also was getting a little tired shlepping my karaoke machine around. Every time I lifted it, I felt I was giving myself a hernia and not getting paid for it.

Just about that time I got a call from my cousin, Elayne Stein, who is a drama coach in the Phoenix area. She knew about my show business aspirations and told me about a new cabaret musical that was auditioning for singers.

I told her I'm a comic, not a singer, and I really don't think it makes sense for me to try out. She said, "Don't be a wimp, give it a try."

I went to the audition with my friend, Paul Jennings, who was visiting with us from Akron, Ohio. I needed him for support but he wasn't much support! He was more nervous than me.

There were about thirty men and women at the theater that night trying out. I met the producer/director Peggy Lord Chilton who had performed with the show off-Broadway in New York City. I chose "Just a Gigilo" as my song. I sang it up-tempo, waving my arms all over the place and moving up and down the stage.

When I finished there was a smattering of applause. My friend Paul was shouting and whistling "one more time." I told him to knock it off. It was only a tryout.

The producer/director Peggy Lord Chilton (I really like saying that name) asked me to sing another song, preferably a ballad and not to wave my hands about so much. She said, "Keep your hands in your pockets while you sing and stay in one place."

I stuck my hands in my pockets and asked the piano accompanist (Flora Mogerman) to play "Embraceable You." I started to sing and did the first chorus with my hands in my pockets. Then I just stopped singing, looked around and said, "Plums? When did I buy plums?"

Everyone broke up and started laughing. I figured I blew it. Peggy Lord Chilton said to me without batting an eye. "Don't call us, we'll call you." (The oldest cliché in the world.)

My friend Paul left town and I completely forgot about the audition. About a week later when I came home from playing golf, Gloria told me that Peggy Chilton called. She said, "Peggy wants you for one of the leads!"

I had to start rehearsals in two weeks. I got really nervous. I had never done a musical and really had difficulty remembering lyrics. I told Peggy Lord Chilton it took me twelve weeks just to remember the words to "Bye, Bye Blackbird."

We had our first rehearsal meeting and I met the seven other members of the cast. There were five women and three men plus Flora, our musical conductor. That was in 1997. We were told that we would do no more than two weekends at the Stagebrush Theater, a nice, small venue in Scottsdale.

I was given forty songs to remember, seven solos and the rest of the songs were ensemble productions. I went into total shock! There was no way I could digest all those songs.

I worked like a dog trying to memorize the songs. Most of the cast had training in musical theater. They really helped me in preparing for the ensemble numbers. Previous to auditioning, I had made plans to go golfing in Ireland with three of my friends. I certainly wasn't going to cancel the trip. It was all paid for and I really needed a break from the rehearsals. I took all the musical arrangements with me on the trip to memorize.

One of our stops was in Killarney. We stayed at the Killarney Inn, a small hotel that was absolutely beautiful. I shared a room with one of my golfing buddies, Jim Morgan. He has a personality that, when he leaves a room, it lights up. He comes across like a real miserable bastard.

In real life, he's a great guy. Most people who play with him complain bitterly about him. I always tell them that he isn't really like that. Jim found out I was telling people that he is a good guy and told me not to do that. He wants people to think he's miserable, then they don't bother him.

Every chance I had, I went over the songs and lyrics for the show. We went to sleep after having a few drinks and I fell asleep like some one clobbered me. I got up to go to the john about 3 a.m.

and then got back into bed. I couldn't fall asleep again, so I began to go over one of the ensemble songs, "I'm Glad I'm Not Young Anymore," from the musical, *Gigi*.

I was humming and singing very quietly (my golf buddies were all gentiles), but the next morning when I went down to breakfast, Don Gates, one of our foursome, was waiting for me in the lobby. He said, "Jim didn't sleep a wink last night because you kept him up all night singing!"

I asked, "Why didn't he say something?"

Don said, "Well, he said he didn't want to interrupt you because he thought you were doing some kind of ancient Hebrew chant."

The next evening I was sitting in the lounge with Don. He was helping me rehearse and I was singing a love song to him. Two Irishmen looked in the lounge and were about to come in when they saw me singing to Don. Don kept saying to me, "You gotta put more feeling into it."

The two Irishmen turned around and couldn't get out of the lounge fast enough! Although I did hear one of the Irishmen say that he thought Don was pretty cute.

I finally got back to rehearsals. We had two weeks until opening night. Everyone was working their butts off. We rehearsed from 6 p.m. to midnight every night, including weekends.

The show started to come together but I was still having difficulty remembering many of the lyrics. I didn't mention we also had to do dance routines along with the songs.

On opening night we played to a sold-out house. I kept peeking through the stage curtain counting the people. It was very exciting! Just before our opening number the right side of my chest started to burn and itch at the same time. I was singing, "Look At That Face" from "Stop the World" to one of the female singers in the show. She happened to be having some dental work done at the time and one of her teeth was missing, so there was a gap on the right side of her mouth.

I was going out of my mind with my skin itching and burning. I was trying not to scratch myself and was concentrating with all of my power looking right into her mouth and singing the lyrics, "Look at that face, look at that beautiful face...Look at that space in your face."

I honestly didn't realize what I was singing. The cast cracked up laughing and I just kept scratching and singing. I couldn't wait to get off the stage.

Opening night of the Senior Class was fantastic. What started out to be a five performance show went for five years and over 350 performances. I finally got to the doctor and was diagnosed as having "shingles," which is generally caused by stress. Ha! And all along I thought I was a calm person.

Anyway, I had a great time working with the cast of "The Senior Class." Everyone in the show had wonderful talent. My first paycheck came to five dollars and sixty cents. My wife and I laughed for two hours every time we looked at the check. After five years of performing in the show, I decided to leave the show to try my luck at stand-up comedy.

Note: "The Senior Class" is still doing performances around the Phoenix area and getting standing ovations.

Yuma (a true story)

A couple of years ago, I went to Barnes and Noble in Scottsdale, Arizona to do some research on humor. I approached a salesperson and asked her where the humor section was.

Barnes and Noble in Scottsdale is a very large store. She pointed to an area and said, "Go straight down this aisle, turn left, and at the end, you will see the *Yuma* section.

I thanked her and proceeded down the aisle she instructed, then made a sharp turn which put me in front of the Arizona section. I thought to myself, "Why would she send me to the Arizona section?" I thought perhaps the books on humor were mixed in with the Arizona books.

I started to look over the books, but to my dismay I couldn't find any on comedy and humor. However, there were a lot of books in that section on Yuma, Arizona.

I retraced my steps until I found the same salesperson and said, "Excuse me, Miss, I asked you for the humor section!"

She replied, "That is where I sent you, sir. Didn't you find books on Yuma, Arizona there?"

I said, "I certainly did, but I wanted books on humor and comedy."

She started to laugh and then asked me, "Where are you from originally?"

I said, "I'm from New York, but what does that have to do with anything?"

She replied, "I thought you asked about Yuma...but...you meant humor as in comedy."

I looked at her and said, "Yes, that's what I asked for!"

She replied, "When you asked me, with your New York accent, it sounded like Yuma."

I told her, "It must be because of my accent," and we both laughed!

Note: If I'd been at the Barnes and Noble book store in New York City, they never would have sent me to the Yuma section!

The Oldest Comic Standing

What goes around, comes around. I did five years performing in the Senior Class musical in Arizona. Five years doing one show is a long time and last year I was getting antsy to get back to comedy. I was ready to start doing stand-up again.

Mark Mashino, the agent who did the the bookings for the Senior Class agreed to represent me. I also decided to do some advance publicity for my act.

Johnny Sarno, one of the male singers in the Senior Class, and I decided to work together whenever we could. We both liked working with a piano accompanist so we hired the pianist who worked on the Senior Class.

When I did a solo, my act usually ran about an hour. I only did about thirty minutes when I worked with another act to do an hour show.

It was a lot easier doing a shorter show for two reasons. One reason was that I felt my material for the act was stronger if I did a shorter show. Another reason was that I had a fear that I wouldn't remember all the material in the act if it was too long.

Often, when I did a show, I would make up large cue cards with the material written on them. My wife would always sit in the front row or table and hold up the cards. People always asked if it helped but I told them it was just very comforting to me knowing the cue cards were there.

During that year, while I was performing at a dinner theater in Sun City, Arizona, a strange thing happened. I was doing my regular act and started to tell a joke that I had done hundreds of times. (See "Natasha" in the Favorite Jokes chapter.)

When I reached the punch line, my mind went totally blank (a senior moment). There was a hush in the room. You could hear a pin drop. My wife, Gloria, sitting next to the stage gave me the punch line but because the room was totally quiet, the people in the entire room heard it.

The audience went wild. People came up to me after the show and asked if she was part of the act!

For a long time I always opened my act with the story of how I forgot the punch line. Then, I would come on the stage with a local newspaper and pretend to read an article from the paper.

I'd greet the audience, then say, "Research says that two out of three people who live in Scottsdale are ugly!.. Now if you don't believe the newspaper article...look to your left. ...Now look to your right. ...If they look pretty good…"

Hmmmmm! That always got a big laugh.

I teamed up with a good friend, Dennis Eynon. He has a wonderful voice and a great stage presence. We took professional photos, put together a promotional letter including a five- minute video and did a mailing to anyone we thought would book us. We got a good response and took some bookings.

The year 2003 was a good one for me. I did eighteen single stand-ups and worked with Dennis on a few more shows. We rented a venue ourselves, hired a band and did a two-night pre-Christmas show with the Arizona Choral Singers that was directed by Dennis's wife, Carolyn, the director of the Chorale. We advertised in the local papers and had a sold-out house both nights. After paying the band and the cost of of the theater rental, we came out pretty good.

After that success, we were on a roll, and thought we should extend our horizons to get more bookings. Dennis sent our promotional videos to the cruise lines. After a few weeks he called them to get their reaction. He spoke to a young woman who told him she liked what she saw on our videos but thought we were too old for her audiences.

Dennis was crushed. I told him she was off base, and that most people who go on cruises are older because who else could afford them? (I finally got us a booking on the Titanic—that'll show her. Ha!)

The Restaurant

Several years ago, I attended a conference in Chicago with my son, Jeff. We stayed at a very nice hotel. After we checked in, we had dinner and retired for the night.

In the morning, when I went down to the desk to meet my son, there was a commotion going on. Jeff was complaining to the manager that he found a roach in the bathroom of his hotel room. He caught the roach in a glass and brought it with him for proof.

The manager apologized and gave him a free night at the hotel. Jeff brought the glass with the roach in to breakfast at the restaurant in the hotel. I asked him why he brought it with him and he answered, "Well, that worked so well to get me a free night at the hotel, I may set up a program to rent a roach!"

Of course, he was kidding, but I never forgot that story.

Recently, my wife and I went out to dinner to a very popular local seafood restaurant with friends. After being seated, our waitress introduced herself. Her name was Kate, and she reminded me of Fran Drescher from the TV sitcom, *The Nanny*.

We ordered drinks and she brought my wine in a little carafe. She poured about a quarter of the little wine bottle into my glass and then said, "I'll give you a few moments to decide on your main course," and she promptly left.

I poured the balance of my wine into my glass. Just as I was about to take a sip I noticed something moving in my drink. I passed my glass over to my wife and said to her, "Do you see something in my drink?"

She said that she did. At that moment, our waitress returned to our table.

I asked her, "What is that bug doing in my wine glass?" She looked in the glass and said, "I believe it's doing the backstroke."

We all laughed and she said, "I'll bring you another glass of wine." She returned with the glass filled to exactly the same spot as the glass she took and before I could say anything, she left.

I remarked to my friends, "I wonder why she didn't bring a fresh carafe of wine?" It seemed as if she brought my glass back to the bartender, they took the bug out and returned the same glass to me that they had taken.

When Kate returned, I mentioned to her the possibility that the bartender may have sent back the original glass. She flipped out and said, "I never would do something like that!" Then she grabbed my glass and said, "I'll take the wine charge off the bill," and she walked off in a huff.

At this point, I really got upset, called her back and said, "Not only do I want a glass of wine but I want a full carafe."

She realized that she had stepped over the line and immediately became very apologetic. She said, "I'll bring you a new glass of wine and please don't be upset with me. I'm having a bad day and taking it out on you."

I said, "All I want is my wine and my dinner. I'm sorry you're having a bad day and I really don't want to upset you but I would like to have my bug back."

Her reply was priceless. She said, "I can't give you back the bug because he's in rehab!"

I told her I would put this story in my book if she would give me her full name. She told me her name was Kate and said, "I don't want to give my last name because I don't know how much longer I'll have it."

We all laughed, paid the bill and left. (Note: The bug in the glass gave me the idea that my son came up with years back in Chicago, but trained bugs are not that easy to come by.)

Today, I have finally realized my dreams. I performed in a musical, did stand-up comedy professionally and now I've completed my first book. The frustration I had drove me to take many different roads to get into the business, and now my lifelong dream has become a reality. (I think it's the time for me to make a comeback!)

A long time ago, when I gave one of my 8-inch by 10-inch glossy prints of myself to my mother, I wrote on it, "It's never too late!"

I want to thank everyone who read my book. I hope you got some laughs from it. I would like to leave you with this simple thought that I usually close my shows with:

YOU'RE BORN...YOU WATCH TELEVISION... AND YOU DIE! AND IF YOU'RE LUCKY...YOU GET GOOD RECEPTION!

This book has been a tribute to all the comedians, impressionists, actors, humorists, writers and friends who have given my life such wonderful moments. It was a privilege to see and hear these talented people. Over the years, they have generated much laughter in my life. Read the following list of names and see how many of these laugh-makers you remember.

Remember the old saying: When you laugh, the world laughs with you. Cry, and you cry alone.

Appendix

COMEDIAN LISTING

Milton Berle
Lucille Ball
Phyliss Diller
Red Skeleton
Jackie Mason
Jack E. Leonard
Al Bernie
Al Nessor
Jan Murray
Corbett Monica
Rodney Dangerfield
Billy Crystal
Don Rickels
George Burns
Gracie Allen
Jack Benny
Phil Harris
Bobby Sargent
Jack Carter
Charlie Chaplin
Don Adams
Ronny Martin
Norm Crosby
Fred Allen
Steve Allen
Robert Klein
Alan King
Dick Shawn
Jean Carrol
Henny Youngman
Mel Brooks
Howard Morris
Carl Reiner
Sid Ceaser
Jonathon Winters
Art CArney
Jackie Gleason
Jerry Seinfield
Jay Leno
Robin Williams
Bob Newhart
Bob Hope
Tim Allen
Dave Barry
Charley Callas
Morey Amsterdam
Rich Little
Danny Gans
Frank Gorshin
Mac Robbins
Mal E. Lawrence
Woody Allen
Whoopie Goldberg
Pat Henry
Jackie Miles
Shecky Green
Larry Best
Bobby Ramsen
Myron Cohen
Sam Levinson
Eddie Murphy
Belle Barth
Harvey Stone
Buddy Hackett
Pat Cooper
Richard Jeni

Red Buttons
Richard Pryor
Lenny Bruce
Joey Bishop
Larry Storch
Martin & Lewis
Dick Gregory
Eeorge Carlin
Dick Capri
Jackie Vernon
Freddy Roman
Bill Cosby
David Steinberg
Dean Murphy
The Slate Bros.
The 3 Stooges
Laurel and Hardy
Arnie Rogers
Louie Nye
Richard Belzer
Drew Carey
Ray Romano
Jim Carrey
Elayne Boozler
Dana Carvey
Dave Chappel
Bill Maher
Tom Poston
Dennis Miller
Ellen Degeneres
Joan Rivers
Bob Saget
Chris Rock
Danny Kaye
Martin Short
Steve Martin
Rita Rudner
Walter Matthau
Richard Lewis
Dave Letterman
Peter Sellars
George Gobel
Gary Shandling
Joe E. Lewis
Tom Poston
Harvey Korman
Stan Dubrow
Larry Bronsen
Harry Stern
Jason Alexander
David Frye
Jackie Winston
Elayne Stein
Connie Alderman
Imogene Coca
Groucho Marx
Harpo Marx
Nanette Fabray
Chris Kattan
Tina Fey
Rachel Dratch
Carrol Burnett
Tom Conway
Allan Sherman
Marty Feldman
Dom D'Louise
Mr. Ballantine
Johnny Carson
Gilda Radner
Frank Fontaine
Foster Brooks
Herb Shriner
Jerry Lester
Frank Gorshin
Ron Carrey
Dave Barry—author
Martin Shore
Mort Sahl
Martha Raye
Michael Richards
Jackie Kanan
The Ritz Brothers
Joey Adams
Danny Thomas
Neil Simon
Jack Carson
Jack Lemon
Jon Lovitz